LOOK GOOD NAKED

THE BATTLE FOR A BETTER BODY has been a very personal journey for Melbourne-born Donna Aston.

Fifteen years ago and 20 kg over her present weight, Donna stopped listening to the overwhelming flow of poor or biased or downright untrue information and began her research into the areas that have become her lifelong passions: health, fitness and nutrition. Five years later, she put her knowledge into practice, transforming her body through exercise and diet, and going on to represent Australia in numerous international body-shaping competitions.

In 1995, Donna became the first Australian to earn

professional status in this area. She has represented Australia in Atlanta, New York and, most recently, at the 1999 Ms Universe Competition in London, in which she placed sixth.

From the pudgy dieter drowning in the sea of weight-loss myths and propaganda, Donna had transformed herself. And she was ready to share her secrets.

Donna's passion led her to a career as a personal trainer. She has worked with hundreds of clients, all the while studying every piece of information about weight loss, nutrition and exercise that she could lay her hands on. With thirteen years of research and experience under her belt, Donna decided to make her unique, holistic approach available to everyone. And so Donna's first book, *Fat or Fiction*, was born.

In creating *Fat or Fiction* Donna hoped to outline a way of eating that would provide optimum nutrition and thereby alleviate many of the symptoms and the results of an unbalanced diet. These include excess body fat/obesity, suppressed immune system (resulting in recurring viruses, etc.), skin problems, diabetes and hundreds of common ailments. *Fat or Fiction* was taken to heart by Australians and went on to be an outstanding bestseller.

Donna knew that *Fat or Fiction* was capable of providing women and men with the bodies that they had always wanted. However, she wasn't prepared for the vast amount of feedback and the myriad requests for more: more information, more structure, more recipes, more on exercise – more! And so her second book, *Body Business*, was born.

Like *Fat or Fiction* before it, *Body Business* also struck a chord with Australians and was soon a bestseller. Donna continues to be inundated with feedback and requests for more information. Her third book, *Stayin' Alive*, was released twelve months later, again to an overwhelming reception.

Donna and her British-born husband, Adrian, now spend most of their time in Australia where she continues to train clients ranging from the 'boy next door' to Australian celebrities. She still dedicates time to sharing her realistic solutions to weight control, dieting and healthy ageing, and she is persistent in campaigning against dishonest, profit-inspired weight loss shams.

For more information about Donna, and her work, please visit her website at:

www.DonnaAston.com

DONNA ASTON

LOOK GOOD NAKED

MyoKinetics™ –
the art of deep tissue toning

important note

The information and recommendations in this book are based on
the assumption of good health and the absence of physical ailments
and illness. If you are currently under the care of a medical practitioner
or have any injuries, I strongly recommend that you seek professional
advice before making changes to your exercise and diet regimen.
If taking prescription medication, always consult your physician.

Published by Hybrid Publishers
Melbourne Victoria Australia

First published in 2002

National Library of Australia Cataloguing-in-Publication data:

Aston, Donna.
Look good naked : *MyoKinetics* the art of deep tissue toning.

MyoKinetics™ is a trademark of Donna Aston

Bibliography.
Includes index.

ISBN 1 876462 26 4.

1. Physical fitness - Handbooks, manuals, etc.
2. Exercise - Handbooks, manuals, etc. I. Title.

613.71

Edited by Linda Roach
Designed and typeset by Ellie Exarchos
Photography by Christian Wild
Illustrated by Glenn Willowsmith

acknowledgments

Firstly, I would like to thank my publisher, Louis de Vries, for having confidence in me and trusting my judgment – it's good to be home!

Linda Roach – a great editor, advisor, creative director and all-round buddy – thank you for being patient, always having time and only being a phone call away. Your contribution to every aspect of this book is priceless (as always).

Ellie Exarchos of Scooter Design – what can I say? Four books and four great covers – you are brilliant!

Christian Wild – thank you for the wonderful photographs and being an absolute pleasure to work with.

To my friend, Glenn Willowsmith – thank you for the time, effort and passion that you put into creating our clever little illustrations.

Andrew Lock – the best physiotherapist ever! Thank you for your continued support over the past decade, and for your kind contribution in this book.

A big thank you to Jillian Bowen of EPR for helping to create awareness of my work in recent months. Sig and Tom ... your encouragement and advice is invaluable. I'm a lucky girl – thank you so much.

Thank you to my loyal readers and clients who continue to inspire and motivate my work.

And last, but certainly not least, thank you to my husband, Adrian – I love you.

Do you feel comfortable in your birthday suit?

For many of us, the 12-week season we know as summer can be a body-baring hell. The images of tight, sleeveless tops, bare midriffs, VPLs, gaping shirt buttons and winter belly bulges begin to hurtle through our minds at a frightening rate of knots. We spend the cosy winter months rugged up in our 'secure' woolly clothing, then the temperature starts to rise; perhaps a move to Antarctica is considered.

I, for one, remember sweating profusely in long trousers and sleeves on many a hot summer's day, all in an effort to disguise a body that I felt uncomfortable with. The mere thought of baring my legs in skimpy shorts or, heaven forbid, my whole body in nowhere-to-hide swimwear, sent my 'cringe-factor' soaring way off the graph!

Too many of us are disturbed by the sight of our own naked reflection, let alone subjecting our bodies to the scrutiny of others. The consequent anxiety rates pretty highly – equivalent to that of singing solo on stage and going for your driving test, all rolled into one! How do you cope? Shunning invitations that risk another human catching a glimpse of your bare skin? Dressing in shapeless, yet skilfully concocted outfits, ducking every time a camera comes into view?

But what if you could be so proud of your body that you could wear any outfit you please, with confidence. I'm not suggesting that you have the desire or inclination to walk around naked in public, but if you look and feel good out of your clothes, you'll look and feel fantastic in them! No more smoke and mirrors, and camouflage. It's not simply about losing weight, being 'thin' or having a 'perfect' body. It's a matter of taking pride in *your* body and providing it with the exercise, care and attention it deserves. To diet and simply lose weight often leaves us without tone or shape, not to mention probably unhealthy. The last thing we want is to look like emaciated 'coat-hangers'. But what if you could 'look good naked' with confidence?

contents

Foreword xii

PART ONE: The body revolution

MyoKinetics The ultimate body management system 3

Chapter one The evolution of *MyoKinetics* 5

Chapter two What makes *MyoKinetics* different? 9

– Who will benefit from *MyoKinetics* 11

– Moments of madness – fitness fairy tales exposed 13

Chapter three Self-made (wo)man 19

– The birds and the bees 20

– The Schwarzenegger complex ... men, women and muscle 23

Chapter four Body by design 25

– So, what exactly is mind-muscle connection? 26

Chapter five *MyoKinetics* – The basic principles 31

– Core stability and posture 31

– Skill vs. brawn 34

– The process of deep muscle toning – no pain, no gain? 40

PART TWO: Crafting your greatest work of art

Chapter six Week one: mind...meet body 49

 — Muscle groups and *MyoKinetics* familiarisation tasks:

back 51

chest 54

shoulders 56

arms 58

abdominals 60

butt 65

legs 70

Chapter seven Week two: muscles in motion 74

How to stretch and lengthen individual muscles 74

MyoKinetics basic push-up 80

MyoKinetics basic squat 82

MyoKinetics reverse lunge 84

MyoKinetics tricep dips 86

MyoKinetics 'ab trio' 88

MyoKinetics bridge and tuck 92

MyoKinetics skaters squat 95

Chapter eight Week three: pulling it all together 97

– Progressive levels of intensity 97

– The most effective, time-efficient fat burning methods to complement *MyoKinetics* for optimum fitness, definition and tone 100

– Workout one 105

Exercise 1: *MyoKinetics* squat/lunge 106

Exercise 2: *MyoKinetics* push-up and burpee 116

Exercise 3: *MyoKinetics* bridge and tuck 124

Exercise 4: *MyoKinetics* ab trio 132

– Workout two 140

Exercise 1: *MyoKinetics* skaters squat and rear lunge 140

Exercise 2: *MyoKinetics* three-point crunch 148

Exercise 3: *MyoKinetics* bridge and tuck 152

Exercise 4: *MyoKinetics* tricep press and cat stretch 160

– Workout three 168

Exercise 1: *MyoKinetics* plyometric squat 170

Exercise 2: *MyoKinetics* ab 'squeeze and crunch' 178

Exercise 3: *MyoKinetics* plyometric push-up and cat stretch 181

Exercise 4: *MyoKinetics* glute bridge and stretch 186

foreword

Another gem from the Donna Aston collection.

Having known Donna for many years I was not surprised that her books have been such a great success. I was captivated by her first three books, *Fat or Fiction*, *Body Business* and *Stayin' Alive*. I always wondered, though, when was she going to let you in on those secrets that took her understanding of health, nutrition and anti-ageing to its pinnacle, when she used it to shape her world class body!

I've trained with Donna, and over the years I've seen, firsthand, the spectacular changes she has brought to those men and women lucky enough to be her personal clients. In fact I had some concerns that former clients might get together and try to let the secrets out before Donna did!

Fortunately those secrets are here revealed for all of you, for the first time, by the person who created them. Donna has always been a person who wants the answers, and she shares this passion with her clients and her readers. You can feel that energy as you read this book.

I work from a scientific background in my own practice as a physiotherapist, and I have used the principles of *MyoKinetics* with my own clients to great effect.

Donna has taken the essence from the years of exercise skills that she has learned and taught, and she has created a highly effective and efficient exercise program. But the real secret, the vital ingredient is Donna's mind-muscle connection. She teaches her readers to focus on specific muscles to perform specific tasks. That is the key to the success of *MyoKinetics*.

Whether I am treating a high powered executive with little time for fitness or a professional athlete who trains all day, time efficiency and results are the gold standards of today's society. *MyoKinetics* gives you both.

I now understand why Donna has placed *Look Good Naked* as her fourth book and not her first. The life changing dietary revolution she began with *Fat or Fiction* continues now with *MyoKinetics* – the science of physical change.

Those of you who are familiar with Donna's work already know of the tremendous results that await you. Those who are new to Donna's work are in for a life-changing experience.

Andrew Lock, B (Physio), Cert. MDT, CFCE(USA), MAPA

Andrew Lock is a physiotherapist with extensive sporting and fitness experience. He has worked internationally, and is a current judge for the International Federation of Bodybuilders. He is sports medicine editor for *Australian Ironman* Magazine, and physiotherapy consultant and internet forum moderator for Aussie Bodies. Andrew has worked with a diverse range of athletes including Australian Test cricket players, AFL footballers, professional skateboarders, martial artists and fitness athletes. Andrew is widely sought after for consultation on spinal and sporting physiotherapy and has a private practice in Melbourne, Australia.

PART ONE
the body revolution

MyoKinetics
The ultimate body management system

The dilemma these days is not whether to exercise or not, but which form of exercise to choose. It would be difficult to find an individual who is not aware of at least some of the benefits of exercise. There is no getting away from it: we live in a society where obesity and its related diseases are rapidly increasing.

We are spoiled for choice and yet, from my many years of training people and talking to people who want to be healthy, and from the countless people who have contacted me since my first book was published, I am acutely aware that there is confusion and dissatisfaction.

Pilates, yoga, weight training, aerobics, water aerobics, step, pump, cardio funk, spinning, rev-master, RPM, boxacise, cardio, kick boxing, tai chi, tae-bo, cardio burn, body combat, boot camp ... I'm exhausted already! Some methods can be quite daunting, yet let's face it, all we really want is to keep it simple. We want to find the most effective method of getting into shape, preferably without hefty time commitments, mantras or contortion!

Meet *MyoKinetics* – a revolutionary body management system, designed to achieve muscle tone and shape, coordination, flexibility, stamina, optimum breathing, fat loss and injury prevention. Most importantly, *MyoKinetics* is about developing an acute awareness of your body by learning how to focus your mind on the individual muscles that you want to exercise, thereby creating deep tissue tone and achieving the most effective and efficient result possible. This is the mind-muscle connection: switching off 'autopilot' and consciously 'driving' your body. Once you have learned the skills and practised the techniques presented in *Look Good Naked* you can apply them to the home workouts that are taught in this book or to any other form of exercise to reap greater benefits.

Rather than focusing on exercising longer, faster or heavier, *MyoKinetics* frees you to exercise 'smarter'!

chapter one

The evolution of *MyoKinetics*

Knowledge is power

I have spent the past 20 years experimenting with weight training and fitness methods in an attempt to improve my personal health, fitness and body shape. For the last 15 of those years I have been doing the same for others.

I started off in the gym. Or, more accurately, gyms! I spent much of my late teenagehood erratically switching from gym to gym – first mustering up the motivation and confidence to go, and then trying to find one that would hold my attention span for longer than two workouts!

As I'm sure you are aware, gyms and health clubs can be pretty intimidating places. Within the fitness industry there are two distinct stereotypical gyms – the 'serious, bodybuilding' type and the 'posher, fitness-recreational' type. As a female and a novice, I was almost always drawn to the latter, purely because I found the serious gyms downright scary!

I did eventually find a gym in which I felt comfortable and I actually began to experience what it felt like to *really* train my body. It was a truly exhilarating experience, although I still felt a distinct lack of control over the direction of my progress. This is when I began to refine my exercise by continuously deciphering variations of basic movements in a quest to develop the most efficient methods.

During the next few years, I explored numerous forms of exercise, including pilates, yoga, gymnastics, stretching and ballet. Much to my surprise, many of their basic 'core' movements bore some resemblance to those that I had adapted to my regime. Each one of these methods had its benefits, yet I still felt that I had not found the 'complete' workout, and there certainly wasn't enough time in the day to do them all! As my knowledge and proficiency grew, I began to experiment, combining the most compelling principles of each method with my increasing knowledge of physiology and body movement.

From this foundation, I began to gain some pretty phenomenal results. I could hardly believe my eyes when my body began to show significant signs of improvement, and in all the right places! By this stage, I was inundated with requests for personal instruction in my seemingly unusual, but indisputably successful technique.

With a couple of years of consistent exercise under my belt, I decided to challenge myself to a body-shaping competition and that year, placed fifth in the World Championships. Over the next five years, I continued researching and refining my program and became the first Australian to earn professional status in fitness / body-shaping competition. As if this wasn't enough, I had also qualified to represent Australia in the inaugural 1995 Ms Olympia Fitness competition in Atlanta, Georgia – a dream come true. Much to my delight, I found myself standing on stage amongst all of the women who had inspired me when I first joined the gym. I felt as if I'd stepped right into the pages of one of my favourite fitness magazines!

As many of you die-hard gym junkies know, it's a pretty rare thing to achieve a dramatic transformation of your body shape. With my well-honed knowledge of deep tissue toning, I became increasingly frustrated to see enthusiastic people dedicating countless hours to the quest for a better body, without success. You see it's not the amount of hours you spend exercising, but the quality of your exercise! I am now notorious for spending very little time exercising, which often leads people to the conclusion that I am just genetically gifted or lucky. Well, let me tell you, when lean, firm bodies were being handed out at birth I was nowhere to be seen! When it comes to exercise, some of us seem to struggle like mad to achieve mediocre results. For this reason, I was inspired to fine-tune my techniques to such a degree that optimum results are achievable and sustainable – *quality, not quantity!* Of course, what you choose to do with all the other hours of the day is pretty important too.

Fairytale: *You must spend countless hours a day exercising to gain benefits …*

Fact: Scientists at the Oklahoma State University in the US tracked 79 000 people for a year. They discovered that those who exercised for just 20 minutes twice a week were significantly less likely to call in sick to work than non-exercisers.

How does exercise combat germs? Researchers at Texas Christian University in the US measured the immune system cells and found that people who exercise have significantly higher counts.

As diet, nutrition and inner health have been the focus of my previous books, *Fat or Fiction, Body Business* and *Stayin' Alive*, now I think it's time to complete the picture with a bit of 'panel-beating' for shape and tone. Whether you are a die-hard gym junkie or a couch potato, *MyoKinetics* will provide you the knowledge and motivation to get results!

MyoKinetics is a unique method of mind-muscle connection: learning to switch off 'autopilot' and 'drive' your own body. This is a skill that evolves from a sound understanding of your basic anatomy and mechanics, ultimately producing the most proficient and effective means of sculpting your body. No matter what your chosen exercise method, from weight training at the gym to the exercises outlined in this book that can be performed anywhere, without the valuable skill of *MyoKinetics* your results will always be inhibited.

chapter two
What makes *MyoKinetics* different?
Mind over matter

MyoKinetics focuses on creating heat and energy while minimising wasted effort. It targets specific muscle groups to achieve deep tissue toning.

Based on 20 years of research and 'in the field' experience, this program provides you with a 'user-manual' for your body: your body becomes your exercise equipment. The *MyoKinetics* workouts presented in this book incorporate the essence of the most valuable principles of the best exercise methods. The result is a time-efficient, result-oriented regime that can be performed anywhere, anytime and by anyone at any level.

Using a unique method of deep muscle toning, *MyoKinetics* incorporates a user-friendly combination of flowing, yet intense movement. The results? A time-efficient, gravity-defying, metabolism-boosting regime! The good news is that all you need to achieve this is your own body! Most importantly, you don't have to leave home to become an expert. That's right. To master *MyoKinetics*, you don't need to purchase complicated, expensive equipment or gym memberships. This book provides you with a complete home-workout regime, which eliminates the necessity for travelling back and forth to the gym or fitting in with class schedules.

The technique that I will teach you in this book will become a personal asset that will enable you to reap optimum benefits from the time and effort you put into improving your body – anytime, anywhere. By developing an acute awareness of your mind-muscle connection, you will be able to isolate and focus your efforts towards individual muscles and muscle groups. This unique level of control will enable you to choose the specific areas of your body you wish to improve at any given time.

Many of you, I'm sure, will be relieved to know that you can achieve results without backbreaking workouts and heavy weights. Unfortunately, to date, most workouts that exclude weights have been a rather flimsy, second-best alternative. *MyoKinetics* doesn't just match the efficiency of working with weights, it is capable of surpassing it! Whether you're a football player or a classical ballerina, you will get more from practising *MyoKinetics* than from any form of exercise you have experienced before.

Who will benefit from *MyoKinetics*?

The workouts in this book have not been designed for those who wish to become heavily muscled bodybuilders. For such extreme muscular development, one would almost certainly require the addition of very heavy weights (amongst other things!). *MyoKinetics* is, however, unparalleled for developing substantial deep tissue tone. Rather than increasing muscle 'bulk', this toning effect will actually form lean tissue into compact packages of firm and shapely contours, actually 'down-sizing' your overall appearance. The *MyoKinetics* principles will help you to achieve that 'long and lean' look, combined with improved strength, flexibility, poise and posture.

Those of you who are accustomed to using weights as resistance may find it difficult to come to terms with a complete regime that requires little more than your body weight. Contrary to popular belief, regular weight training often has a tendency to make us a little lazy, relying completely on lifting dumbbells and bars to force our muscles to respond. However, once you have mastered the mind-muscle tasks, you can apply your new skills to your current weight-training regime. This will inevitably increase the intensity of your workouts and the results will be evident. You only need to observe gymnasts and ballet dancers to realise that heavy weights are not necessary for developing superior tone.

My former gymnastics coach had never picked up a dumbbell in his life, but his level of muscular development and definition was nothing short of inspirational (okay Shannon, don't get a big head!). I did challenge him to a workout with weights on one occasion and of course, he excelled. His control and focus became obvious as he tuned-in to his muscles and executed every movement like a pro! As my coach during intense preparation for body-shaping competition, he convinced me to quit weights to further advance my gymnastic skills. The results were quite remarkable. This experience allowed my body to graduate to another level. My skills improved and I began to develop a strong sense of body awareness.

What results should you expect?

Those of you who have read my previous books will know that to achieve optimum shape, tone and definition you must make the best food choices and add some cardiovascular exercise. Combine this with *MyoKinetics* and you will truly begin to see your body change quite dramatically. You will be performing your *MyoKinetics* deep tissue toning regime three times a week. In addition, I recommend the following:

1. *Beginners* fat burn optimiser: walking for 20 minutes on alternate days (i.e. 4 days a week).

2. *Intermediate* fat burn optimiser: walking EVERYDAY for 20 minutes at an intensified pace.

3. *Advanced* time-efficient fat burn optimiser: in conjunction with an intensified 20-minute daily walk, invest in a skipping rope. Skipping will be added to your *MyoKinetics* intervals, as outlined in your schedule in later chapters.

Like anything in life, you will get out of this what you put into it. The time commitment necessary to achieve total body conditioning through *MyoKinetics* is minuscule – less than 2 per cent of your week, to be precise! There are 168 hours in each week. No excuses! I'm only asking you to commit a maximum of three of these to make significant improvements to your body shape, health and state of mind.

Moments of madness – fitness fairytales exposed

Before embarking on a new exercise regime, it is important to have an understanding of exactly what specific exercises can, or cannot, do for you. This will not only help you to set realistic and effective goals for yourself, but you will be less likely to waste your valuable time and money on inappropriate memberships, gismos and gadgets.

Many of the myths and misconceptions surrounding exercise are so established that I have even encountered fitness professionals who seem duped by the deceit of these 'fairytales'.

There are now almost as many exercise fads as there are diets, boasting amazing claims to whip us into shape. There appears to be an endless flow of new gadgets on the market and, not unlike diet fads, the advertising is telling us exactly what we want to hear. Having been in this industry for almost 20 years, I think I've heard it all. We've tried to melt and wobble our way to toned, buffed physiques. Let's take a moment to reflect on some of the more popular moments of madness, which, ironically, appear to be the most ludicrous!

- ➲ Large comfy beds with hinged moveable sections so that you can exercise while you relax and read your favourite magazine.
- ➲ Gadgets that you strap onto chosen body parts to give you electrical impulses that somehow magically 'melt' away

your fat, leaving you 'toned and slender'.

- ➡ High-tech plastic wrap (garbage bags) that you stick to your
  thighs, in which you run around the park in an effort to
  'sweat-out' the fat.
- ➡ Vibrating belts that are strapped around your bottom
  (usually in public) to cause ultimate humiliation whilst
  'wobbling' the fat away.
- ➡ Plastic cling film that is wrapped around you in
  gorgeous salons and based on the same wonderful logic as
  the garbage-bag principle, just a lot more expensive.
- ➡ Foul-smelling poultice that is caked on your body, the
  claims amounting to somehow 'leach' the fat from
  beneath your skin.
- ➡ Oxygen bars – a buzz in gyms in Europe and the US for
  a while, encouraging members to breathe scented fresh air
  to increase energy levels … at a price, of course.

There have been so many mail-order fitness gadgets that it would be impossible to mention them all: the ab master, the butt master, the slide … the list goes on. But you need only scan the weekend classifieds to find out how many are 'as new' and up for resale.

We have been conditioned to expect instant gratification from our exercise efforts. By popular demand, we've had gizmos to measure everything from our heartbeat to calories burned to calories eaten to steps taken and kilometres travelled.

No matter how bizarre, we do tend to go all out for the latest fad. Unfortunately, many of you will know from first-hand experience, that they usually fizzle-out pretty quickly when you get bored, or over-do it and injure yourself. You soon come to the realisation that your new regime ain't all it's cracked up to be!

Weird and wonderful workouts

For some more amusement, think about some of the more entertaining concepts, invented purely to capture our exercise attention span – at least until the next one comes along. It seems that the only prerequisite for popularity is that a Madonna has tried it!

We'll start with the gazillion styles of yoga. Now I'm certainly aware that many traditional forms of yoga provide great benefits, and have done for centuries, but don't you think that the marketing gurus have taken this ancient culture and milked it for all it's worth? Let's see what a bit of 'westernisation' has created:

- medieval yoga (performing postures while holding candles!)
- disco yoga (too many flashbacks and way too much spandex!)
- inflight yoga
- office yoga
- bedtop yoga

What next? Scuba yoga? Or perhaps supermarket-checkout yoga? Why not? They've already invented underwater tai chi … don't forget your snorkel!

Another one that takes my fancy is 'kareoke spinning'. I know you think I'm just being silly now, but it exists! I'm not sure if you'd be in tune while trying to 'sing n' spin', but it seems to be a popular choice in La-La land.

How about a spot of bellydancing? Tushy-shaking Shakira, popular singer, has sent the popularity of bellydance fitness skyrocketing as she belts out her hit songs. There is actually a rather extravagant beginner's video available, demonstrated by twins Veena and Neena!

Jane Fonda set the pace as the 'aerobics queen' of the 1980s. Her spandex-clad body inspired us to jig around the loungeroom like there was no tomorrow. In a similar era, Australia's own Olivia Newton John got 'physical', introducing an unsuspecting public to fitness fashion statements such as towelling headbands and woolly legwarmers.

'GI Jane' or 'boot camp' workouts seem to have taken the fitness world by storm. I think a bit of discipline can go a long way, but have we lost the plot when we pay money to have an angry army drill sergeant hollering abuse in our ears at 5 am?

'Hulacise' – no hoops involved here, but rather, a lei! This intriguing concept incorporates a bit of Hawaiian tradition, including a warm up with chanting.

The 'goddess workout'. Explanation escapes me, so I'll just quote the website description. 'Enjoy the rhythm of a live drummer and flautist while Goddess Dolphina brings veils and other mystical props to teach you hip shaking, tummy tightening and belly dance moves.' Say no more!

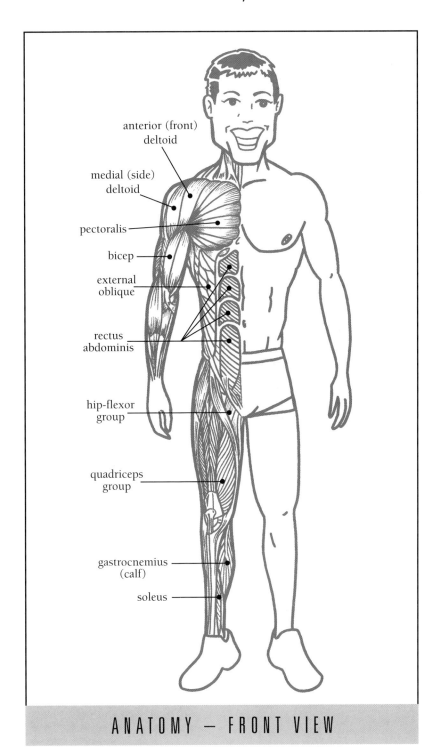

anterior (front)
deltoid

medial (side)
deltoid

pectoralis

bicep

external
oblique

rectus
abdominis

hip-flexor
group

quadriceps
group

gastrocnemius
(calf)

soleus

ANATOMY — FRONT VIEW

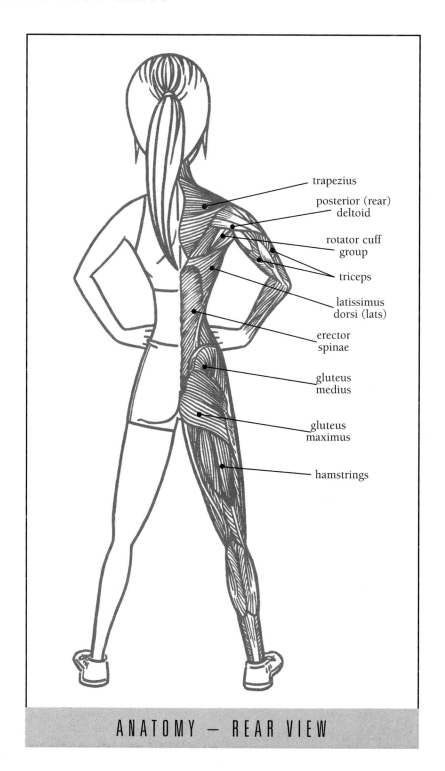

trapezius

posterior (rear) deltoid

rotator cuff group

triceps

latissimus dorsi (lats)

erector spinae

gluteus medius

gluteus maximus

hamstrings

ANATOMY — REAR VIEW

chapter three
Self-made (wo)man

'Everyone is self-made, but only the successful admit it!'

Having made dramatic changes to my own body, I know that with the right knowledge and focus, you too can significantly change your body shape.

The 'key' factor in toning and sculpting your body is body composition: your ratio of fat to muscle. It is of utmost importance that you have a solid understanding of this concept before you can make any exercise program work for you. My readers will already have an understanding of just how important body composition is in improving your appearance and health. How many times have you heard people use genetics as an excuse for having wide hips, thick thighs, narrow shoulders, fat knees and ankles – you name it – our gene pool has been lumbered with the lot! Of course, we all have various genetic traits that are manifested in our bodies, but ultimately, our lifestyle choices dictate our physical condition. When we accept this we can no longer shirk our responsibility for creating change. I'm often told that I'm so 'lucky' to be in the shape I'm in, but believe me, luck has nothing to do with it. Before I started exercising, I had very narrow shoulders, which only emphasised my rather generous hips, bottom and thighs. My legs were an unfortunate 'carrot-shape' (you know the look) and by the time I was in my teens the saddlebags had begun to protrude and my cellulite was developing at such a rate that it was actually visible through my trousers. If you take a look at the front cover, I think you'll agree that I've made some significant changes over the years, completely transforming what I once thought was my 'genetic shape'. If I can do it, so can you. Let me tell you how it's done …

The birds and the bees

Besides some obvious variations, men and women possess basically the same skeletal structure. For example, the length and width of our bones vary, dictating our height and basic frame size. As the female body matures, childbearing capacity causes the hipbones to be wider set than those of a man. The muscles that are attached to the bones are composed of thick, elastic fibres strategically placed so that when they are signalled by our brain to contract and extend, they move our skeletal structure with precision and ease. Between our skin and our muscles is a layer of insulation and reserve energy known as stored body fat. The distribution of fat cells (fat storage tanks) in the body varies in each individual. When we remain lean, the distribution of this fat layer appears quite even. If we begin to gain an excess of stored body fat, the areas that house the majority of our 'storage tanks' increase significantly and become noticeably uneven.

You will have noticed that during the prepubescent years the physical structure of boys and girls is very similar. As we begin to mature, hormonal changes create a more obvious distinction between the muscle mass, body fat distribution and general masculine/feminine characteristics. Due to a naturally higher level of the male hormone, testosterone, men have a much higher level of muscle mass than women. Male hormones also play a primary role in body fat distribution. As a general rule, men have a lower percentage of stored body fat than women, but when they do gain fat, it is usually around the mid-section, often leaving the limbs comparatively lean. The primary female hormone, oestrogen, influences the amount of body fat we store, as well as how our fat is distributed. The typical 'female' areas for excess fat storage are between the waist and the knees, and often the back of our upper arms … isn't nature cruel!

Women have a lower level of lean muscle tissue than men. So lack of exercise, the wrong exercise and/or the wrong diet, often lead to a narrow upper body in comparison with lower body proportions. The reason that our hormones encourage this 'extra padding' is related to childbearing. Patiently anticipating pregnancy, women's bodies still have a very primitive urge to retain enough 'reserve energy' (body fat) to sustain a pregnancy during stints of famine. This instinct for preservation explains why our menstrual cycle is often interrupted if our body fat levels fall very low (commonly experienced by athletes, ballerinas, etc.), and why the task of reducing our body fat sometimes seems to be quite daunting. A woman's body is not at all keen to be super-lean! This is another reason why restrictive fad diets *can't* work. A woman's body can be very frugal when it comes to surrendering body fat. Any threat of famine (which is what your body thinks is happening when you eat less than you need) will cause an instinctive switch to 'starvation mode'. Your body will then hoard fat stores – hence the all-too-common plateau, followed by the dreaded yo-yo syndrome. You cannot outsmart your body … it will beat you every time!

Understanding that hormone levels play a significant role in the physical condition of both men and women makes us even more aware of the importance of maintaining our health with regular exercise and a good diet.

We can send our hormone levels haywire by allowing our bodies to become over-fat and out of condition, further hindering fat loss and muscle gain. I hope that you can now begin to see the significant influence that regular exercise can have on our shape, body composition and health.

Fairytale: *You must consume copious quantities of carbohydrates to give yourself energy to train …*

Fact: We are bombarded with manufacturers' advertisements claiming that their processed grains and sugar-laden treats are specifically 'engineered' as athletes' 'fuel'. Some of them are endorsed by athletes. Don't be fooled! Some athletes would endorse the consumption of white bread soaked in cordial if they were paid enough! Any athletes who believe that these 'food imitations' are genuine, become just as disillusioned as other knowledgeable consumers once they do their research. As I have stated in my previous books, highly processed foods do not contain any viable nutritional value. Sure, you need more calories if you are engaging in regular intense exercise, but what you require is quality not simply quantity! If anything, when you push your body to its limits, you require a far higher standard of nutrients from your food than the average, sedentary person. Many athletes excuse their poor eating by boasting that they just 'burn it off'. While they may not be gaining excess body fat from these empty calories, their health, energy and consequent performance will suffer, sooner or later.

The Schwarzenegger complex ... men, women and muscle

A misconception that seems to be quite prevalent is that resistance training will make us increase in size or gain too much muscle.

You may be surprised to know that the majority of the population is actually 'under-muscled'. That's right. Over the past 15 years I have measured the body composition of thousands of men and women, only to conclude that very few actually have adequate, or 'normal' amounts of lean body mass. In fact, on average, most are between 5 and 10 kilos under-muscled.

Unfortunately, the mere mention of the word muscle often conjures up ideas of bulging biceps and 'bulky' physiques. In actual fact, most of us are not carrying the normal, minimal amount of lean tissue to sustain our metabolism, let alone being in danger of increasing our overall size due to an excess! Building any muscle tissue is a difficult and slow process and certainly not one that happens by accident. Even if you are *trying* to gain muscle, you are unlikely to gain more than a couple of kilos of good quality, lean tissue in a year. So if you are 5-10 kilos below your ideal level, you've got some work to do! By not carrying enough muscle tissue on your frame, you will experience a significantly impaired metabolic rate. Consequently, you will not only be faced with a steady gain of excess stored body fat, but you will also find it extremely difficult to lose fat.

chapter four
Body by design

Mind-muscle connection and body awareness …
learning how to isolate muscles and sculpt your body shape

I have explained the concept of 'body composition', your lean to fat ratio, in great detail in previous books. Here I will offer a simple analogy: your body and a gold wedding band. As a wedding band increases in carats of gold, the 'size' of the ring doesn't increase, but rather, the composition changes. We are aiming to change the composition of your body and increase its 'quality'. An increase in lean tissue and a decrease in body fat will create a positive change in your body composition, leading to a significant improvement in your appearance and general health … regardless of how much it all weighs on the scales. In fact, muscle tissue weighs more than body fat, so it is possible that you will 'shrink' in size, yet remain the same weight. The visual result is a body that looks and feels toned, strong, energetic, lean and healthy.

The bottom line? Through the deep tissue toning effect of *MyoKinetics*, you will increase your muscle density (as opposed to size), boosting your metabolic rate and allowing you to burn more calories – '24/7' – even while you sleep!

Developing a sound understanding of the mind-muscle technique is the foundation of successful and proficient practice of *MyoKinetics*. Although this may seem like a strange concept now, there's nothing 'airy-fairy' about it. It will enable you to consciously select one muscle at a time, feeling and visualising its full range of motion. Hmmm – I thought that might get you and your bottom-muscles excited!

Part of the way through my extensive study of human movement and physiology I realised that, subconsciously, I had always used this technique, which helps to explain the comparatively rapid results early in my training. Training countless clients over many years has enabled me to develop and refine the principles of *MyoKinetics*.

So, what exactly is mind-muscle connection?

It is a learned skill that evolves from a sound understanding of your basic anatomy and mechanics. Mastering it may prove a little frustrating at first, but stick with it and practise the familiarisation tasks ahead – you won't believe the incredible effect that this skill can have on your body shape.

Basic mechanical movements, such as squatting or raising your arms above your head, are usually initiated by your subconscious. Rarely do you consciously contemplate which muscle you will use to perform specific exercises, let alone everyday tasks. Most of us are on permanent autopilot! With a strong mind-muscle connection, you can consciously change the muscles that have been subconsciously selected to perform any physical movement. Now, of course, you cannot use your biceps to move your legs, but you can choose your glute (bottom) muscles to dominate the majority of lower body movements (such as squatting), as opposed to the often-stronger quad (thigh) muscles. This is only one example where a switch in focus can be used to take pressure off your knee joints, and reshape your bottom and trim down your thighs. The wonderful thing about developing this skill is that you can balance the strength and tone of weaker muscle groups while performing everyday tasks, as well as during specific exercise moves. The subconscious repetition of habitual movements and the autoselection of specific muscle groups, will cause your body to develop certain strengths and weaknesses that make it susceptible to injury, and joint wear and tear. These subconscious movements also play a significant role in your body shape … or lack of it! Harnessing the mind-muscle connection offers the most proficient, effective means of toning and sculpting your body. It also has another very valuable asset; it brings you a genuinely renewed interest in exercise – no more boring repetitions! Learning to 'drive' a body that you have lived with all your life is challenging and captivating and, best of all, it will respond with incredible results. The more you know about the anatomy of your body (see illustrations on pages 17 and 18), the better your awareness will be.

In a nutshell … the mind-muscle connection is about learning to switch off the autopilot and 'drive' your own body.

Hands-up those of you who have done weight training in *fits and bursts*, only to find it positively mind-numbing. I often find that even the most experienced training enthusiasts are completely unaware of the precise muscle they are working in any given exercise. Sometimes their guess is not even warm! One of the primary reasons that gym enthusiasts have problems defining specific muscle groups is because they use weights that are too heavy. Not only does this hinder form, but it's also a completely inaccurate method of measuring progress and is unnecessary for deep tissue toning. *MyoKinetics* will enable you to make your muscles work intensely using only your body – no weights, no equipment. Of course, you can also apply *MyoKinetics* principles to your existing weight-training regime to achieve exceptional results.

Let's call a spade a spade

➜ Learning how to operate and use a machine or contraption to facilitate exercise is boring.

➜ Learning how to operate and use your very own body in ways you never thought possible is downright exhilarating!

Most of you probably assume that weight training is essential for defining and shaping our muscles. On the contrary, as mentioned before, the use of dumbbells and equipment is often the 'lazy' way to train. Although they have their place, once you have mastered a sound mind-muscle connection, dumbbells and machines will be the last thing you *need* to have a good workout. Of course, this skill can be applied to weight training if building significant muscle *size* is your goal (or if you happen to enjoy the gym environment).

Whether you are a seasoned athlete or a complete novice to exercise, without the mind-muscle technique, your results will always be restricted. The concept is based on pure physiological fact and once you have mastered this skill, you'll begin to wonder how you lived without it!

Gravity ... the reason we can exercise using our own body weight

Gravity is a powerful force. It spills drinks, emphasises our ageing skin and eventually makes our bottoms sag. But it's not all bad. *MyoKinetics* actually puts gravity to work *for* you, helping you to develop a better body.

Most weight-training enthusiasts will judge their progress by monitoring an increase in increments of resistance. It is very common to reach a plateau, where you seem to no longer reap benefits from or make progress in a previously successful regime. The majority of experienced trainers who have come to me for advice on overcoming a plateau are usually shocked when I reduce the weights they currently use by as much as half! Why such a drastic reduction? Because this is normally what it takes to facilitate correct technique, consequently forcing the muscles to work to their optimum capacity. For example, if the maximum your bicep muscle is capable of lifting is 10 kilos, yet you increase the dumbbell weight to 15 kilos, you will most likely start to use momentum, recruiting surrounding muscle groups to help with the load. In turn, this will put your muscles and tendons at great risk of injury as you lose form to compensate. Your bicep will probably not even be permitted to lift the original 10 kilos (as surrounding muscles have effectively removed much of the intensity), let alone the intended increase!

The foundation of *MyoKinetics* is based on mastering the skills of mind-muscle connection and, from this, developing the ideal form and position for executing specific movements. This powerful combination will guarantee results.

chapter five

MyoKinetics — the basic priciples

Hone your skills and condense your efforts for deep tissue tone

Core stability and posture

The deep-lying supportive muscles of the abdomen, pelvic floor and lower back provide us with a 'girdle' of strength and stability as we perform exercises, as well as everyday tasks. By strengthening these muscles and learning to 'switch' them on when our body requires their support, you are acquiring a most valuable asset. These muscles should be involved in most everyday movement, providing 'functional' strength and reducing the risk of injury. Whether you are reaching for a glass from a tall cupboard, lifting shopping bags or simply walking, they are working overtime! If they are neglected and allowed to deteriorate or become 'lazy' we become vulnerable to injury, unnecessary wear and tear, and pain and stiffness. Lack of core stability is unnecessarily taxing on other muscles that are not equipped to handle such responsibility but are

31

recruited by the body to compensate. Core-stabilising muscles are aptly named because their function is just that – to provide a stable 'base' for smooth, safe movement.

Toned to the 'core'

The advantages of strong core stability are seemingly endless, from improving sporting techniques to injury prevention in common daily activities as well as in sport. A recent Canadian study showed that golfers who tighten their abdominal muscles at the start of their swing experience less back pain than those who don't.

We've got no excuse when it comes to perfecting core stability, because the familiarisation exercises necessary for mastering it can be carried out all day, everyday. Whether you are at your desk, in a monotonous board-room meeting, walking, driving your car or watching TV, mastering core stability is a cinch. In fact, you don't even need to put down this book to start! Sit up straight, ensure your pelvis is in a 'neutral' position (not forward to cause a 'sway' in your back and not back to cause slouching, but rather a central position). Once your pelvis is in correct alignment, you will find it impossible to slouch forward. No 'banana backs' here – just try it! Don't cross your legs as this will tilt your hips out of position and consequently destabilise your alignment and overall posture. Okay, now we have two things to remember for optimum core stability and good posture:

1. Sit down and set your pelvis in a 'neutral' position. Imagine that a piece of string has been attached to the inside of your navel and that it is being pulled from behind you, drawing your navel towards the vertebrae of your spine. This movement should be subtle and isolated only to this specific area. If anyone nearby notices what you are doing (apart from your expression of deep concentration!), then you're using way too much movement. This is an 'internal' movement that activates the deep stabilising muscles of your abdominal area and is crucial to core stability. But it is in no way a strenuous movement. Practise this exercise several times a day, everyday, until it becomes second nature to employ these muscles as you begin any *MyoKinetics* movement. Once these muscles have been educated to act on reflex you will achieve a superior level of overall muscle control, posture and poise. As a result, you are providing your body with a powerful tool to protect against injury and degeneration.

2. Imagine that you have a helium balloon attached to the top of your skull and it is gently pulling you upwards, stretching and lengthening your entire torso. This posture allows you to breathe deeply and freely, takes pressure off your digestive organs and intervertebral discs, improves circulation and allows your supporting postural muscles to relax, naturally loosening muscle stiffness and tension.

My gymnastics coach, the delightful Shannon, had a unique method of drumming this concept into my skull. He would place me in a handstand position, with my feet against the wall for balance and a stopwatch between my hands where I could see it. For one full minute, my body was to remain as 'tight' as a plank of wood. He would then push and prod me in my torso, and try to pull my feet apart to make me aware of any weaknesses in my stability. This drill aimed to teach my mind and muscles to endure a state of 'sustained contraction'. Please don't try this at home! I was at my peak of physical conditioning and, even then, I wouldn't recommend it. In hindsight, it was actually rather sadistic, but it certainly taught me core stability in a big hurry!

I soon discovered that the majority of movements in gymnastics and classical ballet are impossible without this skill, as it is an integral component of balance, strength, propulsion, control and ultimately, injury prevention. *They* make it look so easy, but when you gain a first-hand understanding of the level of difficulty involved in the incredible gravity-defying balance and control exhibited by these athletes, you soon realise that they are true masters of core stability. You will also notice that their general poise and posture are second to none – in and out of the competitive arena. I am not suggesting that we all have the talent or inclination to become Olympic gymnasts, however, I am suggesting that we can learn an awful lot from these basic principles and use it to great advantage in our everyday life.

Skill vs. brawn

An interesting test of core stability is the single-arm push-up. I used it to conduct a little experiment, the results of which were astonishing. You see, I thought that the obvious skill required to perform a single-arm push-up would be upper body strength, but I was proven wrong. Of course, some upper body strength is required but it all boils down to – you guessed it – core stability. I challenged some of the 'big guys' at the gym to perform a single-arm push-up, but I'm sad to say that I left a trail of deflated egos in my wake! These are men who can 'bench press' in excess of their own body weight, so they each certainly qualify as 'Superman' in my book. Incredibly, some of the biggest, strongest guys were incapable of performing one single-arm push-up. Why? Because the primary requirement is core stability, which facilitates even weight distribution. Without the support of super-tight core muscles the body is allowed to 'sag' as the second arm is removed from the floor. The arm that is left is placed under too much pressure, rendering a smooth push-up action impossible. Most of the guys were mystified and dejected when they watched a couple of the smaller girls find the task relatively simple. Sorry for letting the cat out of the bag boys – it was, after all, a scientific experiment!

Fairytale: *If you quit resistance training, your muscle will turn to fat …*

Fact: Once you learn about body composition, you realise that this statement is physiologically impossible. Muscles are living, working tissue and play an essential role in moving our bodies around. Body fat is excess energy that our body has stored as a reserve for later use. In other words, fat and muscle are very different tissues made from different cells. One cannot magically 'turn into' the other. As I have said many times, it would be like a fingernail turning into an eyeball – it can't happen! This myth stems from the fact that you lose muscle tissue when you stop exercising so your fat burning capacity decreases.

The bottom line?

➔ We stop exercising

➔ Our muscle tissue deteriorates from lack of stimulation

➔ We continue to consume the same amount of calories that we did when
we were active

➔ Decreased muscle, combined with an excess of calories = increased body
fat storage.

So often I have heard disillusioned ex-athletes excuse their slip from their former physical prowess by claiming that their 'once so-developed' muscle has somehow deflated and gravity has reduced it to dangling loose muscle that they just can't get rid of. Sorry, we're not buying it!

Isolation and compound movements

The *MyoKinetics* workout will provide you with a balanced combination of both isolation and compound movements to achieve optimum deep tissue toning. In each familiarisation task in the following section there will be an indication of whether it is an isolation or compound movement. Put simply, an *isolation* movement usually involves just one joint and therefore allows isolation of a specific muscle or muscle group. This muscle or muscle group can then work to maximum intensity with far less resistance and very little involvement of secondary supporting muscles. This is where the mind-muscle connection proves to be an invaluable tool, enabling you to isolate muscles, facilitating precision shaping of specific body parts and reducing stress on joints and tendons. Isolation movements create an acute awareness of your body, which helps to reveal any imbalances or weaknesses it may be harbouring. This, in turn, helps reduce the risk of injuries.

In contrast, *compound* movements involve the use of two or more joints, therefore calling upon various groups of supporting muscles to complete a movement. Again, your mind-muscle connection is a crucial factor in reaping maximum benefit. Compound movements are necessary to strengthen many of the smaller supporting muscle groups that are often overlooked in isolation movements. These muscles facilitate 'functional strength', providing an advantage in everyday tasks such as bending, lifting and climbing stairs. Compound movements play an integral part in developing a substantial body-shaping foundation. They offer stability and protection to our joints and connective tissue, as well as assisting the development of balance, posture and core stability.

Breathing

I realise that it may seem odd to remind you of a bodily function that is supposed to be involuntary. Of course, if conscious thought were a necessary part of respiration, I think it would be safe to say that life expectancy would fall significantly! Many of us unconsciously hold our breath at times of exertion and this can be dangerous, as it robs our body of oxygen at a time when it is most needed. For this reason, breathing correctly during exercise is something we need to become very aware of.

How many of you have actually thought about why you yawn, apart from being tired? When we are tired our breathing is shallow. We also yawn when we are not tired but our breathing is insufficient. Think about it – what happens when we yawn? That's right – we involuntarily inhale a deep breath of oxygen. So, if you have noticed that you yawn sometimes during exercise it is because you need to breathe more deeply. And all this time you thought that you were just bored!

There really are no precise rules when it comes to breathing during exercise – as long as you are! I try to encourage people to breathe as naturally as possible, but it is often difficult to breathe in upon exertion or when your body is curled forward restricting your lung capacity. In these situations, I suggest that you exhale upon exertion (e.g. when pushing yourself away from the floor in a push-up). When performing abdominal exercises that require a curl forward, I suggest that you exhale as you curl forward, and inhale as you return to an extended, relaxed position. If completing a more lengthy set of exercises that requires multiple breaths, be aware of your breathing and try to relax by inhaling full, deep breaths through your nose and exhaling through your mouth. Again, posture is of utmost importance to efficient breathing so don't slouch as you exhale.

You might find yourself 'running out of puff' while performing strenuous exercises such as skipping or running. You must be conscious of your breathing technique throughout such activities. Inefficient breathing will certainly lower your endurance. Many people expel oxygen each time their foot hits the ground. This is a common error in breathing while performing activities that involve impact (i.e. running, skipping), and results in shallow breathing. You must learn to breathe completely 'out of time' with your running or skipping rhythm. Focus on breathing deeply and efficiently, regardless of your stride.

Joint angles and the art of muscle selection

An important factor in mastering your mind-muscle connection is being able to visualise basic joint mechanisms. By becoming familiar with the angle of a specific joint, you will begin to develop the ability to shift focus from one muscle group to another within the context of the same movement. For example, if a squatting movement is performed *without* mind-muscle focus your body will automatically select the strongest muscle group to execute the movement, which, in this case, would be the quads. (Of the lower body muscles, the quads [thighs] are usually the most dominant.) Increasing the angle of your hip joint and decreasing the angle of your knee joint, will intensify this movement and cause your body to recruit the muscle fibres of the glutes, over and above those of your thighs. I repeat: this form of mind-muscle visualisation is the key to *MyoKinetics* and optimum deep tissue toning.

The function of joint angles will be indicated in exercises in later sections. The primary joints involved in the movement of our major muscle groups are the shoulder and hip joints, both of which are 'ball and socket' joints, and the knee and elbow joints, both of which are 'hinge' joints. Due to their unique structure, ball and socket joints are capable of moving in a multitude of directions, consequently involving quite a few of the larger muscle groups that act as 'prime movers', as well as many underlying stabilising muscles. The structure of the hinge joint is similar to that of a door hinge, in that it moves in a restricted plane, making the isolation of surrounding muscle groups relatively simple. The knee joint is a hinge joint. You don't need me to tell you that it is not designed to bend backwards or move in a circular motion. A basic under-standing of joint angles together with proficient mind-muscle skills will provide you with the ability to lengthen tight muscles, enabling better joint mobility and ultimately, facilitating the *art* of muscle selection.

The process of deep muscle toning – no pain, no gain?

Most of us have experienced muscle pain to varying degrees, but the common belief that we cannot make progress in the absence of 'pain' is misleading. Firstly, most of us can distinguish between the pain of mus-cle fatigue and soreness related to exercise, and the pain associated with injury, which is often far more acute.

Fairytale: *No pain, no gain…*

Fact: It's actually the word 'pain' that bothers me. Although I do understand the idea behind this commonly expressed phrase, I often worry that exercise enthusi-asts take it a bit too literally. While I am a big believer in intense exercise once an advanced level is reached, I certainly don't recommend a regime of pain and suffer-ing to anyone – myself included! I'm sure that an experienced athlete coined this phrase, because the type of 'pain' that a trained body experiences is a far cry (par-don the pun) from the pain of injury or over-exertion. An exercise session performed at the appropriate intensity should leave you quite relaxed and exhilarated having conquered your set challenge. If you experience 'pain' beyond a temporary build-up of lactic acid from muscle fatigue, you are out of your depth. If you do injure yourself by overdoing it, I can guarantee that no 'gain' will accompany this 'pain'!

Intense forms of exercise will cause temporary muscular tenderness and stiffness. It is common for that soreness to develop 48 hours after your workout. In fact, it is so common, that there is even a name for it – 'DOMS' – delayed onset muscle soreness. It can be particularly nasty because enthusiastic novice trainers will often dive straight back into a similar workout the following day, only to recognise the full extent of their actions as they try to crawl out of bed the following morning!

While the feeling of muscle tenderness is a normal part of the deep tissue toning process, the degree of soreness we accept as normal is an important factor. During the process of working our muscles, we create tiny 'micro-tears' in the muscle fibres, triggering a repair process. Once this repair process has been repeated several times, your muscles will gradually begin to strengthen and develop greater tone. If you overdo it, or use poor techniques or weights that are too heavy, the overwhelming muscle pain can be a result of more significant tears in the muscle fibre, which can actually be classed as injuries. They will take longer to repair, cause unnecessary interruption to your quality of life and hinder a consistent workout regime. Consequently results will suffer too. So you see it is of utmost importance to pace yourself. If you have a lay-off from exercise for any period of time, take particular care to build up gradually upon your return.

There are many other factors involved in the muscle repair and recuperation process. Your dietary intake and general lifestyle can play a significant role. Your muscles are limited by the nutrients you make available for their growth and repair. Now I'm not suggesting for one minute that you rush out to your local supplier of bodybuilding supplements and grab a bucket of 'massive muscle gainer'. What I am saying is that plenty of 'real' foods, and possibly some supplements, are called for, particularly when you are subjecting your body to physical stress. Of course, if you require more detailed information about food and nutrition read *Fat or Fiction*, *Body Business* and *Stayin' Alive!* The saying 'you are what you eat' is absolutely true … so if it's not good enough to 'wear', don't eat it!

Tools of the trade checklist

Although 'tools' are not necessary for *MyoKinetics*, there are a couple of 'optional extras' that might make completing the workouts in this book a little easier, particularly if you progress to an advanced level.

- Most of the *MyoKinetics* moves are timed. Initially, you can use your watch, or you can purchase a basic stopwatch. Of course, you can rely on your eggtimer if you prefer! You may choose to simply count in your head. The critical element is that you don't cheat on time!

- If you don't have carpet or a mat on the floor, I suggest that you use a firm exercise mat for comfort as much of the exercise involves contact with the floor.

➡   One exercise in the third workout calls for a standard cushion or rolled up towel.

➡   The advanced levels require a skipping rope. This is an inexpensive investment, only required if you choose to progress to that level.

➡   Wear comfy clothing and shoes and have a bottle of water handy.

➡   Last, but not least, your chosen location is important. I recommend a quiet room with no distractions. *MyoKinetics* requires a certain degree of concentration and focus, so sprawling out on the lounge room floor with your head swivelled backwards watching TV is not ideal. The *MyoKinetics* workouts outlined in later chapters are ideal for home, travelling or anywhere that you find yourself with restrictive resources, space and time. The majority of the familiarisation tasks can even be practised in your car, or on a bus or plane. All you need is your body and the skills learned with *MyoKinetics*.

PART TWO

crafting your greatest work of art

MyoKinetics CHART

	Monday	**Tuesday**	**Wednesday**
Week 1	familiarisation task BACK	familiarisation task CHEST	familiarisation task SHOULDERS
Week 2	core exercises + stretching	core exercises + stretching	core exercises + stretching
Week 3	*MyoKinetics* level 1	CV1 (walking 20 mins)	*MyoKinetics* level 1
Intermediate	*MyoKinetics* level 2 + CV2	CV2 (intensified walk)	*MyoKinetics* level 2 + CV2
Advanced	*MyoKinetics* level 3 + CV3	CV3 (intensified walk 30 mins)	*MyoKinetics* level 3 + CV3

Thursday	Friday	Saturday	Sunday
familiarisation task ARMS	familiarisation task ABS	familiarisation task BUTT	familiarisation task LEGS
core exercises + stretching	core exercises + stretching	core exercises + stretching	core exercises + stretching
CV1 (walking 20 mins)	*MyoKinetics* level 1	CV1 (walking 20 mins)	CV1 (walking 20 mins)
CV2 (intensified walk)	*MyoKinetics* level 2 + CV2	CV2 (intensified walk)	CV2 (intensified walk)
CV3 (intensified walk 30 mins)	*MyoKinetics* level 3 + CV3	CV3 (intensified walk 30 mins)	CV3 (intensified walk 30 mins)

chapter six
Week one: mind ... meet body

Let me introduce you to a new acquaintance ...
mind ... meet body!

Let's go through each of the basic muscle groups and find out how they *tick* and how we can now use *MyoKinetics* to sculpt them to perfection! You may find it very helpful to keep referring to the anatomical diagrams on pages 17 and 18 to assist your visualisation.

> **Fairytale:** *If you participate in resistance training, you will become 'musclebound'...*
>
> **Fact:** If this were the case, I wouldn't be able to fit through the doorway! I must say, this would have to be the most common myth of all. For some reason, it is a common belief that our muscles have this incredible capacity to expand out of control! I'm assuming that this stems from the sheer freaky mass we see when we look at professional bodybuilders. To gain this sort of mass, we would need to have been

blessed with some pretty unusual genetics, combined with around 8-10 years of living, eating and breathing the gym, and usually pressing weights in excess of our entire body weight! Ask anyone who has tried to gain muscle size – you don't wake up one morning sandwiched between two giant biceps that just won't deflate … not yours anyway! As muscle develops using *MyoKinetics*, it will become more dense and compact (smaller), a long time before it will increase in size. If you combine your training with the appropriate food choices, you will be reducing body fat simultaneously. The result will be a toned, defined body … no resemblance to Godzilla's little cousin!

How to use this section

To enable you to firmly grasp the mind-muscle connection in relation to each of the following muscle groups, I suggest that you read one section each day for the first week. For example, read 'week one, day one' and practise the familiarisation task throughout that day, as you go about your daily routine – in the car, at your desk, watching TV, etc. The next day you should be ready to move on to 'week one, day two', and so on.

By following this mind-muscle development strategy for the initial week, you will also be conditioning each individual muscle group in preparation for your *MyoKinetics* workout program contained in later chapters.

WEEK ONE, DAY ONE
Muscle group: back

The simple word 'back' describes a complex range of muscles that are involved in postural support. They play a crucial role in improving overall body shape and strength in both men and women. They create the illusion of upper body width, emphasising a smaller waistline and hips.

In this section I will introduce you to your back muscles. You won't believe that you've been living with them for years, yet didn't even know they were there! Our back muscles are often neglected in exercise regimes, primarily because they are 'out of sight'. I first observed this 'out of sight, out of mind' phenomenon at the gym. I noticed that even 'serious' trainers developed their 'fronts' (chest, abs, etc.) more diligently than their 'backs'. They obviously didn't realise that if back muscles are well toned, they give our body shape a whole new dimension, from every angle. Now, I'm not suggesting that you have the need or desire to walk around like the stereotypical bodybuilder with a melon in each armpit; but a little back development goes a long way towards building a complete body-shaping foundation. Aesthetically, flaunting a toned and shapely back is a great asset in that little backless dress, or for the guys, that much admired 'v-taper'.

Keep in mind that your back muscles are primarily involved in 'pulling' your arms in towards your torso. To avoid complicating matters, I will simply explain the general range of movement performed by the basic back muscles and suggest the most appropriate method of engaging them in an isolated movement. We will discuss your latisimus dorsi (lats), trapezius (traps) and erector spinae (lower back) muscles. Just to get acquainted with these muscles, try squeezing your upper arms into your sides as hard as you can … brain … meet your lats!

Maintaining good posture and focusing on 'locking-down' your shoulder blades when performing all *MyoKinetics* movements is paramount. When your shoulder blades are locked into place, they will not be poking out behind you like chicken wings! By allowing this posture to lapse, you are breaking the mind-muscle connection and allowing other muscles (such as your traps) to take over your workout. The primary function of the traps is to shrug your shoulders upwards towards your ears, not unlike the 'I dunno' action I see when I ask clients why they didn't do their workouts last week! Scapula (shoulder blade) instability is a common problem that I observe on a regular basis and one that is soon visibly reflected in your shape and proportion. Whether an athlete or a novice, nobody in their right mind wants sloping, coat-hanger shoulders and a thick neck, so pay attention!

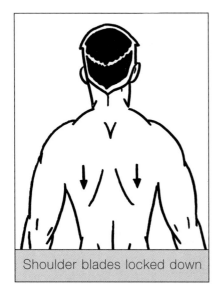

Shoulder blades locked down

Your erector spinae are strong and flexible lower back muscles that play a significant role in correct posture and injury prevention. The erector spinae is one of the major muscles in this region. It is a deep underlying muscle with three 'heads' and it runs the entire length of your spine, from your lumbar region to the base of your skull. This muscle is fully stretched when your body is curled forward, and begins to contract when you lean back, past the usual upright position.

MyoKinetics **familiarisation task**

The task I have chosen for this section will help you to develop good scapula stability and a mind-muscle connection with your lats, as well as a compound contraction of the back muscles.

Compound movement: stand with your back and shoulders touching the wall with your scapula locked into position. With your arms by your sides, bend your elbows and gently press them into the wall, holding for a five-second count. Release and repeat several times. You should feel a general contraction in your upper back muscles.

Practise at every opportunity throughout the day, until you feel that you have mastered the task of familiarisation. Don't be frustrated if you don't feel it in your back muscles straight away. We are teaching your brain a new pathway of coordinated movement and it can take time to feel it in the 'right' place.

Back, elbows to the wall

WEEK ONE, DAY TWO
Muscle group: chest

Technically known as the pectoralis muscles (pecs), the muscle fibres are arranged in a fan-like pattern, which accommodates various angles of movement. Variations in the plane of movement will target different sections of your chest muscles. The primary function of your pecs is to push away from your torso or to draw your arms together in front of you as you would to give someone a big hug! Besides improving hugging proficiency, what other benefits will we reap from good pec development? For the girls, unfortunately no chest exercise can 'lift' or 'firm up' the breast tissue that lies over the top of the pec muscles, however, a developed and defined chest can create the illusion of volume and increased cleavage. Guys, I'm sure nobody will dispute the appeal of a pair of well-developed pecs to round off a balanced physique!

Fairytale: One for the girls … *resistance training will make you flat-chested …*

Fact: I'm guessing that this one stems from observing the extreme physiques of female bodybuilders. Breast tissue is situated on top of our pectoral (chest) muscles and is composed primarily of fat. It is true that the majority of professional female athletes are not very well endowed in the breast region, which is due simply to their extremely low body fat levels. You will notice that this is the case with most very lean females. I have certainly never seen a classical ballerina or a marathon runner with large, voluptuous breasts, have you? Those who defy this general rule of thumb are likely to have engaged the help of a cosmetic surgeon. Anyway, training and developing the muscle tissue that lies beneath the breasts will, in no way, decrease, firm, lift or interfere with the existing volume of breast tissue. Sadly, fat loss will usually cause a gradual reduction in breast size, along with the rest of our fat stores. Some of the 'lucky' girls will have an abundance of fat cells in this area and will still be left with volume once they reach their desired body fat level, however, most of us will sacrifice what we have for a smaller bottom! On the bright side, well-developed chest muscles enhance our overall body shape and posture.

MyoKinetics familiarisation task

Compound movement: let me introduce you to your pecs. One of the most important factors in isolating your pec muscles is correct posture. If you allow your chest to concave or shoulders to round forward, all emphasis is lost. To experience the correct posture, stand with your back to a wall, lock your shoulder blades down and ensure that your head and both shoulders remain in

Chest, back to the wall

contact with the wall surface. With your elbows by your sides, start the movement with your hands beside your chest and slowly push forward with resistance. Imagine that you are pushing a heavy object away from your body and continue pressing through a five-second count until your elbows are straight and you feel a strong contraction in both sides of your chest. Hold this position of sustained contraction for a five-second count before reversing the action. Repeat several times.

It is of utmost importance that you don't lift your shoulders from the wall at any time. When we come to later chapters, you will be performing exercises without the wall for guidance, so try to develop an awareness of this posture that can be carried over to the next stage.

WEEK ONE, DAY THREE
Muscle group: shoulders

Your deltoid muscles (delts) are responsible for much of the broad range of movement of the ball-and-socket shoulder joint. Because of the structure of this joint, your deltoids assist its movement in a multitude of directions. Again, we could go into great detail about the complex movements of the different 'heads' of this muscle, but lucky for you, I'm going to cut to the chase! Nicely developed delts tend to 'square-off' our shoulders, giving the illusion of a smaller waist and hips. They are very aesthetically pleasing as they set the foundation for nicely shaped arms from all angles. Well-developed delts protect our shoulder joints, both in training and in everyday activities. You'll soon discover their function when you first manage to isolate their movement to the point of fatigue. Then just try turning the steering wheel in your car … oh, and you may have to lower all of the cupboards in the kitchen!

Your rear and front delts get quite a bit of work with back and chest movements, so to ensure a well-rounded workout, we will concentrate on isolating the often-neglected side (medial) deltoid.

MyoKinetics **familiarisation task**

Isolation movement: start with your arms by your sides. Make the following movement slow and controlled as you focus on isolating this muscle. You are going to be lifting your arms out to your sides, but rather than focusing on your hands and arms leading this movement, try to visualise the side delt shortening as this raises your arms laterally. Using a five-second count, you'll find it will stop at the point of full contraction, when your elbow is just below shoulder height. Hold this sustained tension for a further five-second count before lowering your arms to repeat the movement. You can increase the intensity of this contraction by gradually turning your thumbs towards the floor as you raise your arms. Remember to keep your shoulder blades locked down throughout the movement to prevent your shoulders lifting towards your ears, otherwise you will be bringing 'traps' into play.

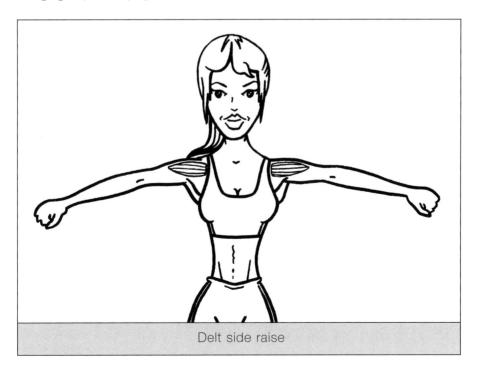

Delt side raise

WEEK ONE, DAY FOUR
Muscle group: arms

Whether toting a briefcase, lifting the kids, carrying the groceries, enhancing your sporting prowess or impressing the pants off your friends, in those sleeveless clothes, strong, toned arms are really quite useful things to have! The two primary muscle groups addressed in this section are your biceps and triceps. These muscles have opposing actions, so while one is contracted, the other is at full stretch. Your biceps are positioned on the front of your upper arm and are responsible for bending the elbow joint, raising your hand towards the front of your shoulder. They also assist the movement of various exercises, in particular, those for the back. The triceps are large horseshoe-shaped muscles situated at the back of your upper arm and you'll feel them contract when your arm is straight. Besides the specific isolation exercises in this section, your triceps are actively involved in various exercises, in particular, those for your chest and shoulders.

The tricep region is a common area for women to store a little excess body fat – you know – you stop waving and your upper arm keeps going! I am often asked for exercises to tone and shape the underlying muscles in this area, which I will address in this section. The most effective way to rid yourself of those 'glomesh handbags' is to reduce your overall body fat by combining regular *MyoKinetics* with a few dietary modifications.

MyoKinetics **familiarisation task**

Isolation movement: you'll be pleased to know that your biceps have a pretty simple range of movement. The elbow is the only joint involved in this movement. It is a hinge joint (remember, it only moves in this one simple plane, as opposed to a 'ball and socket joint'), like those found in shoulders and hips. Your triceps also operate the same simple action of the elbow joint, but in the opposite direction. For this reason, we will combine today's tasks for both muscles. Ensure that your posture is correct: imagine standing up against a wall with your shoulders and elbows touching the surface. To isolate your biceps, rotate both palms up (so that your little finger is closest to your body). Keeping your elbows

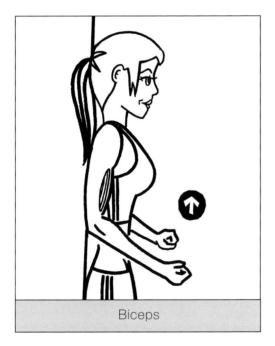

Biceps

Triceps

at your sides begin to bend your arms. Through a five-second count, imagine that you are pushing against the resistance of a heavy object. You will reach full bicep contraction when your hand is at shoulder height. Hold this sustained tension for a further five-second count. At this point, rotate your palms again (thumbs closest to your body) and begin a five-second count as you push down with resistance until your arms are straight down by your sides. Hold the sustained tension at this point for five seconds as you feel your tricep muscles at full contraction. Repeat this task at every opportunity throughout the day.

WEEK ONE, DAY FIVE
Muscle group: abdominals / mid-section (abs)

There are so many myths and misconceptions surrounding ab exercises that I could write another book just about them! Let's begin by breaking the mid-section down into two major muscle groups:

1. rectus abdominis – a large, flat sheet of muscle that extends from just below your chest to beneath your belly button. When you see a 'six-pack', this is the muscle you're admiring! Besides being 'eye candy', the rectus abdominis plays the important role of curling your spine forward, and generally providing support for your back and stability for your entire torso.

2. obliques, internal and external – these muscles run down either side of the rectus abdominis. Their fibres run diagonally, enabling rotation of the torso, as well as bending to either side. They provide a lot of back support and assist in rectus abdominis movements.

Another small underlying muscle is known as the transversus abdominis. It gets plenty of work with the focus of *MyoKinetics* on general core stability.

Fairytale: *Training your abs everyday will result in a flat, toned mid-section ...*

Fact: Harking back to a previous fable regarding body composition, fat and muscle are two very different things. The complex process of 'fat burning' doesn't involve 'melting away' fat by exercising specific muscle groups. I've said this before and I'll say it again: you cannot 'spot reduce' body fat from a specific area by exercising the muscles beneath it. If it is your goal to have a flat, toned and defined abdominal area, you need to do the following:

→ Develop the wall of muscle in this area by exercising it two or three times a week – just as you would for any other muscle group – no more, no less

→ Modify your food choices and increase your cardiovascular, general fat-burning exercise to reduce your overall body fat percentage.

MyoKinetics comes into play here by combining both fat burning and deep tissue toning. You will only sport a toned mid-section when the layer of body fat covering the muscles is reduced, unveiling the toned muscles beneath. As long as they remain covered, you can have the best ab muscles in the world, but you will never see them! This is the key to a toned tum – or anything else, for that matter.

Forget the hype

Because many of us, men and women alike, are so determined to create a flat, toned tummy, we often fall prey to marketing 'gurus'. Let's get this straight, once and for all:

→ You don't need gadgets and gizmos to exercise your abs

→ You don't have to exercise your abs everyday to beat them into submission!

➔ Boasting hundreds of 'reps' is nothing to be proud of. Besides the mind-numbing effect that this volume of exercise must have, your abs are only muscles, which means they cannot contract 100 times without fatigue. If you can do this many reps, you are actually doing the exercise so badly that your abs have recruited several other muscle groups and a bit of momentum, to chip-in!

➔ That urban legend that divides the abs into 'upper' and 'lower' is taken a bit too literally. The rectus abdominis is a single, large, flat sheet of muscle that spans the entire length of your abdominal wall. The muscle fibres all lie in the same direction and the contraction involves the entire muscle, not sections of it. Some exercises may recruit the assistance of your internal obliques, hip flexors and transversus abdominis, which may account for 'feeling' an exercise working the lower abs. The main reason why so many exercisers are keen to isolate the 'lower' abs is because we commonly store more body fat beneath the navel than above it, often leaving 'ab-enthusiasts' with a 'four-pack', rather than that elusive 'six-pack'. Remember, you cannot melt away the fat in specific areas simply by exercising the muscles beneath it.

MyoKinetics familiarisation task

Isolation movement: part one – rectus abdominis

Lying on the floor, bend your knees and bring the soles of your feet close to your bottom. Focus on the vertebrae in your back. Tuck your chin in and through a five-second count, slowly lift each vertebra, one by one, off the floor as your body begins to 'roll' forward. You will find a point of full contraction, and, depending on your abdominal strength and back flexibility, this generally happens as the shoulder blades are lifted off the floor. If you begin to lift higher than this point, your hip flexor muscles (see anatomy illustration on page 17) will take over, taking all focus off the abs and consequently defeating the purpose. Hold this sustained tension for a further five seconds. From this point, slowly reverse the movement, one vertebra at a time, until you are back in the starting position.

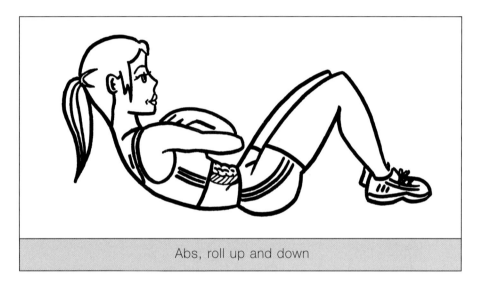

Abs, roll up and down

Isolation movement: part two – obliques

Sitting in a chair, make sure that your hips are not rotated back (see illustration overleaf) so that you set the correct curves in your vertebral column before we begin. It is crucial to keep your hips facing forward throughout the movement. Think of your hipbones as headlights that must remain parallel, 'shining' directly in front of you. The rotation point of your torso is between your ribcage and your pelvis (hipbones), so I want you to slowly turn your chest and shoulders, rotating your upper body to the left. Hold this point of sustained tension for a five-second count and then reverse this movement to the centre (again to the count of five). Repeat on the opposite side. The reason for the return to the centre and pause is to deter you from swinging, or using momentum. There are no prizes for making this a race against time, or accomplishing a huge range of movement. The purpose is to familiarise yourself with the concept of core stability and muscle isolation – slow and controlled.

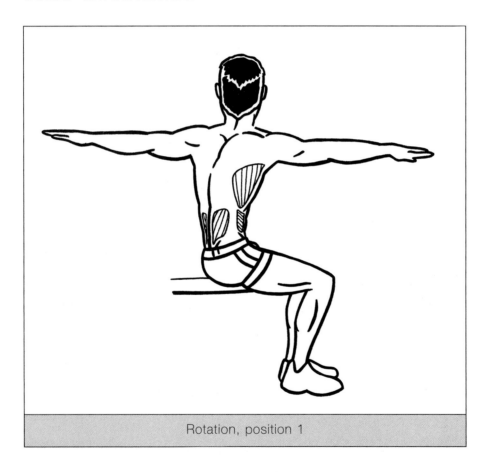

Rotation, position 1

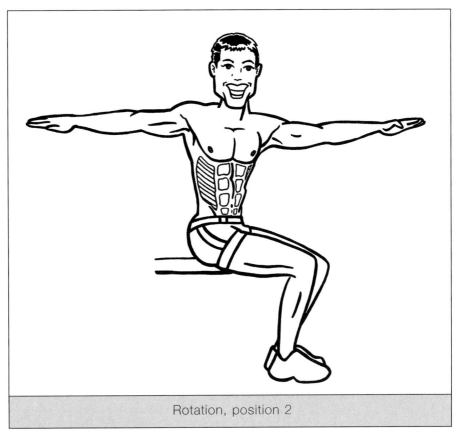

Rotation, position 2

WEEK ONE, DAY SIX
Muscle group: butt (gluteus maximus, gluteus medius)

The action of your gluteus maximus is the primary focus in this section. Its main function is to act as a lever for your legs, pivoting from the hip joint. It is used in everyday movements such as climbing stairs or standing from a seated position. The level of flexibility in your hamstring muscles (in the back of your upper thighs) will determine the range of movement you can safely use when performing exercises that emphasise your glutes. In *MyoKinetics*, we will focus on increasing hamstring flexibility to allow a greater range of movement. Combining your newly acquired skills of core stability, posture and muscle isolation will result in *superior* tushy-tone!

Your gluteus medius is a smaller muscle situated above the gluteus maximus, on either side of the back of your hip. It is involved in the action of your other glute muscles and is also responsible for the abduction (away from the body) and rotation of your leg.

Bottom alert!

The gluteus medius is one muscle that I prefer not to emphasise. I know that there are probably thousands of exercise enthusiasts diligently performing 'cable kick-backs' and the ultimate aerobic-class humiliation – imitating a dog peeing on a lamp post. My advice is to STOP IT! These exercises are shockers. They don't provide any significant isolation for the most important glute muscle, but instead, can over-develop the gluteus medius, creating what I often refer to as a 'veranda-butt'! Simply translated: hips wider than the bottom, which makes the waist appear wider and causes the loss of a certain *peachy* characteristic that we've all grown to admire. If you do go to the gym, steer clear of cable kick-backs and all exercises that involve lifting your straightened leg backwards and/or out to the side, particularly with an externally rotated foot.

Novice and experienced enthusiasts alike are apt to over-develop the quadriceps muscles (in the front of the thighs), simply by exercising on autopilot. It is of utmost importance to develop the glutes, quads and hamstrings equally to avoid injury, so let's start with the largest muscle group and work our way down. I'm a real stickler for technique when it comes to isolating muscles in this group, so bear with me – I promise you'll thank me for the results!

Gluteus maximus

I know, it sounds like a character from a gladiator film, but your gluteus maximus is one of the largest and, potentially, one of the most powerful muscles in your body. Commonly referred to as your glutes (amongst other things!), it spans the entire surface of each butt-cheek – one on each side. Most of us recognise the aesthetic advantages of a well-developed behind, but if the idea of a *tight tushy* doesn't grab you, strong glutes also play the very practical role of protecting your back and joints from injury.

One of the best pieces of advice I can give you regarding glute isolation, regardless of the chosen exercise, is to always push from your *heels*, not your toes, and emphasise the angle of your hip joint, rather than just your knees. Apply this golden rule in every glute exercise you do from this day forward and you'll have a great tush in no time!

MyoKinetics familiarisation task

Compound movement: kneel with your right knee on the floor, bend your left knee at a 45-degree angle and place the sole of your left foot on the floor in front of you (see illustration overleaf). Posture and core stability are crucial in this task, so review the diagram carefully before attempting this movement. Your hips should be rotated to a neutral position to avoid pressure on your back. You might feel a stretch in your hamstring muscle as you make this adjustment. You may use a stable object (chair) at your side to help with this movement until you master it, but make sure this doesn't throw you off centre. Using your front leg, focus all of your weight onto your heel and push yourself directly upward to a standing position, then lower to the starting position. You don't want to lean your body-weight forward or allow your front knee to pass over your toes. Practise several times on each side throughout the day.

Lunge, position 1

Lunge, position 2

COMMON MISTAKES ARE:

➔   tucking your bottom forward. This puts enormous pressure on
     your knees and lower back and transfers the work to your quads.
     Stick your butt out, but maintain core stability!

➔   allowing your 'headlights' to tilt off balance. Keep your hips
     stable and your abs tight;

➡   losing balance. Fix your eyes on an object at standing eye-level and continue to focus on it throughout the movement. This, together with a slow descent, will help to control your balance;

➡   banana-backs! It is crucial to keep your back straight throughout the movement. Concentrate, keeping your eyes focused and chest held high;

➡   holding your breath. Relax and breathe.

WEEK ONE, DAY SEVEN
Muscle group: legs — quadriceps, hamstrings

Your quadriceps muscles are situated in the front of your thighs. 'Quad' refers to the 'four' muscles in this group: rectus femoris, vastus lateralis (externus), vastus intermedius and vastus medialis (internus).

The primary function of this muscle group is to straighten your leg at the knee joint. For the sake of ease, we will refer to this group as the 'quads'. They are, more often than not, involved in movements that I have specified for the butt. In these compound movements, it is your chosen technique that will determine the muscle of focus.

Your hamstring muscles are situated on the back of your thighs, extending from just below your glutes to the back of your knee. Commonly referred to as hammies, they are responsible for bending your knee to curl your heel towards your bottom. They are also largely involved in all compound exercises for the quads and glutes.

In the quest for perfect thighs...

Sadly, I cannot pick up a fitness magazine lately without being confronted by a ridiculous 'inner and outer' thigh regime for *supermodelesque* legs! Now girls, if we want thighs like Elle has, all we have to do is grow a foot taller! But seriously, if you want to improve the shape and tone of your thighs, forget those damned *ab/ad* (abductor /adductor) contraptions. Not only do they make you feel like you've been put up in stirrups, but they do very little to reshape your legs! This machine is supposed to strengthen the abductor (outer thigh) and adductor (inner thigh) muscles, which, at best, may help to condition your legs for sports requiring side-to-side agility, such as tennis, skating or skiing. Unfortunately, the rumour has been perpetuated over the years to promote this machine as a magical *melt-all-of-the-fat-off-your-saddle-bags* contraption. Honestly, how many of you have used this machine for its real purpose of sports conditioning? Hmmm ... just as I suspected. Say this out loud so that you will remember it for life:

Working any muscle beneath an area of stored excess body fat will not 'tone' or 'spot reduce'.

Besides this physiological fact, the abductors and adductors are small, stabilising muscles that come into play in almost every lower-body exercise we do. Without them, we'd fall over! You can't beat the *MyoKinetics* total thigh-conditioning workout for balanced shape and tone.

Although I must admit defeat when it comes to lengthening legs, combining the exercises in this section with overall fat loss will help make legs as close to *supermodelesque* as is possible for us mere mortals!

MyoKinetics familiarisation task

The quads and hamstrings are responsible for opposing actions of the same joint (knee), much like the biceps and triceps are for the elbow joint. In this task we will combine two movements to familiarise you with the range of movement of both muscle groups.

Isolation movement: sitting in a chair, focus on your thighs, contracting your quadricep muscles as you push your feet upwards (as if you are pushing against resistance). Slowly straighten your knees through a five-second count, reaching peak contraction as the knee joints become totally straight. Hold for five seconds and then reverse this action by squeezing the hamstring muscles and bending your knees, using a slow and controlled motion, as if you were pushing against resistance, until your hamstrings reach full contraction when the knee joints are 'closed'. Take a full five-second count to return to this starting position. This is a simple task, even if you are sitting at a desk, or in an aeroplane. In fact, it's a great way to improve circulation in situations where we are forced to be sedentary. Repeat this movement several times throughout the day.

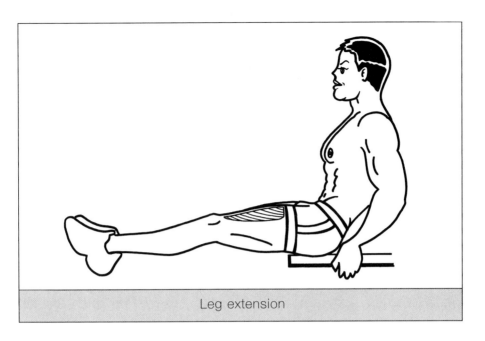

Leg extension

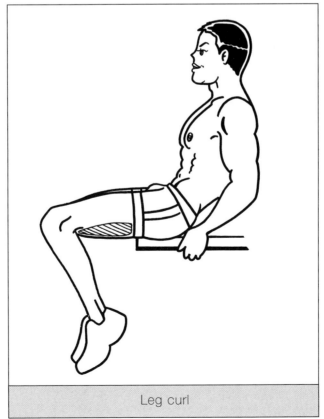

Leg curl

chapter seven
Week two: muscles in motion

Now that you have practised your familiarisation techniques, you are ready to move on to the next phase, which is learning the stretching and exercises that compose final phases. This week, we will apply the isolation skills acquired in the last section to specific muscle movement. In week three, you will have mastered these exercises and will be ready to move on to the final phases of the *MyoKinetics* workout.

How to stretch and lengthen individual muscles

It is now time to discuss the important issues of warm-up and stretching, as they help us to avoid injury, make us aware of our muscles and any ailments, and generally improve the range of motion of individual muscle groups.

Stretching often conjures images of painful, contorted movements.

On the contrary, when done correctly, stretching should be very relaxing. Two aspects of stretching that are important to remember are consistency and relaxation. Successful stretching relieves muscle tension; over-stretching is stressful and may result in injury. Stretching is a great way to gain an understanding of your overall physical condition.

How many of you are willing to admit that you find stretching and warm-up exercises a bit tedious? Yeah, yeah, you know they are 'good for you', but who can be bothered? I have found that most people simply don't want to fluff about before beginning the 'real' exercises, so they often become victims of selective amnesia. You may be pleased to know that for the purpose of ease and time efficiency, I have actually incorporated a stretching component into the *MyoKinetics* workout. This serves four purposes:

- It ensures that we prime and stretch the appropriate muscle group at the perfect time in our workout – immediately prior to any given exercise

- It reminds us to establish the mind-muscle connection before each exercise

- It makes stretching more significant and more closely related to the exercise at hand, which forges a habit that we are less likely to forget

- It becomes far more time-efficient.

  Maybe five purposes – it prevents selective amnesia!

What exactly is stretching and is it really necessary?

Over the years I have found that most people, from athletes to the sedentary, will tell you that they don't stretch as much or as often as they know they should. I think that there are three primary reasons for people's neglect of stretching.

➔   They are not aware of the multitude of benefits gained from regular stretching.

➔   They have not been shown how to stretch effectively, therefore it is often associated with pain.

➔   The less of it they do, the more the muscles shorten and the more arduous the task becomes.

The great thing about stretching, when it is done correctly, is that it feels great! I'm sure that you all have observed dogs and cats stretching instinctively; they look pretty contented when they do. A stretch provides a great opportunity to apply your mind-muscle familiarisation skills. In fact, now that you have this awareness, you'll get a real buzz out of a good stretch!

Stretching actually helps considerably in the quest for a well-sculpted 'bod'. If we don't stimulate our muscles to remain at full length, they won't – it's that simple. Shortened muscles gradually lead to a limited range of movement, which, in turn, inhibits the intensity at which you can isolate any given muscle group. For example, by allowing your hamstring muscles to tighten, you limit the pivot range of the hip joint and therefore the glute (butt) muscles become inactive. Besides the 'gravity' issues, this puts a great deal of pressure on your knees and your lower back as they attempt to compensate.

Other benefits of stretching include:

- ➜ relaxing tension
- ➜ priming the muscle for exercise
- ➜ focusing your mind and reminding you of correct breathing
- ➜ developing body awareness
- ➜ promoting circulation
- ➜ helping the muscles to flush out lactic acid from previous exercise, thus relieving soreness.

The stretch reflex

The first thing you need to know about stretching is that it is not a competition. You don't win a prize for forcing your forehead to touch your knee, or your fingers to touch your toes! There is no pain, suffering or bouncing involved, and if you are trying to force a muscle stretch further than is comfortable, you are defeating the purpose. Just to let you know, our muscles have a 'stretch-reflex'. This means that, thankfully, they are far smarter than we sometimes are! If we force a muscle to stretch too far, or try to 'bounce' a stretch a little further than we can hold, our nerves will try to prevent injury by activating an involuntary reflex action that contracts (tightens) the muscle we are trying to stretch. Unfortunately, some beginners become over-enthusiastic in a quest to increase flexibility – fast. As a result of over-stretching, we may inflict micro-tears in the muscle fibres. They repair by forming stiff, inflexible scar tissue and we gradually become less flexible. Anyone who has experienced this vicious cycle will have unpleasant memories of stretching, perhaps making them pretty reluctant to go through the process of tight, sore muscles again. Well, the good news is, by following a few simple principles, effective, pain-free stretching is a cinch!

Smart stretching

To experience the full benefits of stretching, you must always begin in a relaxed state, allowing smooth movements and easy breathing. Contrary to popular belief, it's all about letting the muscle go, not forcing it to over-extend into uncomfortable, contorted positions. Save yourself a lot of pain and be realistic with your goals and patient with yourself. If it is your ambition to transform yourself overnight, from a couch potato into Gumby, you'll be bitterly disappointed!

One of the first things to be aware of is breathing. It is very common for people to hold their breath when stretching, however, where stretching is concerned, exhalation = relaxation.

The purpose of stretching is to lengthen our muscles, and the angle and position of our joints play a crucial role in this – both in exercise and stretching. It becomes much easier to visualise our muscles stretching and contracting, as we become more familiar with the location and function of each group: mind-muscle connection.

The aim of stretching is to slowly elongate the muscle until you begin to feel *mild* tension. At this point you should concentrate on breathing deeply, relaxing the target muscle and surrounding muscle groups, while you hold the position for 15-30 seconds. As you relax, you should feel the tension gradually dissipate. Don't be discouraged if some days you feel a little less flexible than others. If you have a break from your regime, take care not to jump back in at the deep end as you will have lost some of your flexibility. So take it slowly. There are many factors that can interfere with our level of flexibility. These include temperature, dehydration, inflammation, hormonal changes, lactic acid/stiff muscles and joints, and injury. So learn to listen to your body and be patient.

This week, you will be applying your *MyoKinetics* core principles to some basic exercises, giving you the opportunity to put your new skills into practice. To prime the target muscle group, exercises will often begin with a specific stretch. *MyoKinetics* movements are composed of a timed count to complete the range, coupled with a 'sustained tension' technique to facilitate correct form and enhance the deep muscle toning effect. For optimum results, it is important that you remember your mind-muscle connection and don't rush it!

Each contraction point requires your concentrated effort to incorporate a five-second count to reach the goal position, followed by a five-second count of 'sustained tension', before a further five-second count is used to return to the starting position in preparation for your second repetition. This means that each repetition takes a full 15 seconds to complete.

NOTE:

A repetition: **one full movement from start to finish**

A set: **a group of repetitions performed consecutively**

WEEK TWO, DAY ONE
MyoKinetics basic push-up

Lie face down on the floor. Your core stability is of utmost importance in this movement, so focus on drawing your navel back towards your spine, remembering to breathe naturally while maintaining your core stability. This will maintain your body alignment throughout the movement, preventing a 'sag' in your lower back as you proceed.

Push-up, basic hand placement

Place your hands on the floor, parallel with your shoulders but 10 cm wider. At this point you should feel a gentle stretch through your chest and shoulders. Keep your shoulder blades locked into place and your knees on the ground as you gently lift your 'tight' body 10 cm off the floor.

This is your starting position and you will hold this position of sustained tension for a count of five seconds. Then slowly push yourself further away from the floor and by the count of five you will reach the second position with your arms outstretched. I remind you of your breathing! At this point, immediately reverse the movement for a count of five, lowering yourself to the starting position just above the floor, and hold sustained tension for a further count of five. Remember your familiarisation exercises and make sure that your shoulder blades remain locked down and your posture remains strong. Complete three consecutive repetitions. Practise this set of three twice more throughout the day.

Push-up, position 1

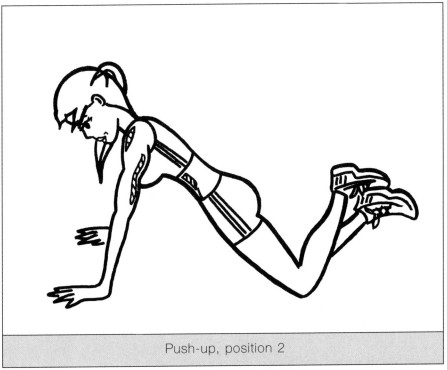

Push-up, position 2

WEEK TWO, DAY TWO
MyoKinetics basic squat

From a standing position with your feet together, step laterally with your right leg so that your stance is 15 cm or so wider than your shoulders. Observe the illustrations opposite before you begin. Remember – don't hold your breath! You must focus on maintaining a relaxed breathing pattern throughout the movement: in through your nose and out through your mouth. If at any stage you are unable to maintain your breathing pattern, you are pushing yourself too hard, too fast. Set your core stability by pulling your navel back towards your spine.

To begin this exercise, cross your arms in front of your chest (like Jeannie, but without the nod!). Remind yourself of your posture and the importance of joint angles in this exercise.

In a slow and controlled manner, bend at the knees and hip to lower your butt towards the floor, keeping your back 'flat' and your weight over both heels. Count out your five-second descent until you reach your goal position (no lower than thighs parallel with the floor). Hold this sustained tension for a five-second count before returning through another five-second count to the starting position. One full repetition must take you 15 seconds to complete. Complete three consecutive repetitions. Practise this set twice more throughout the day.

NOTE: The range of movement you will achieve in this exercise will be determined by your muscle strength and flexibility, so take care not to push beyond your means. The glutes (butt) are the muscles of focus, so the joint angle to emphasise is that of the hips, rather than the knees.

Stretch prior to squat

To facilitate a stretch and prime the muscles for this movement, place your hands on your thighs to stabilise yourself. Slowly bend your knees and hips, lowering yourself into a squatting position. Your thighs should go no lower than parallel with the floor. Hold for ten seconds then push your hands against your thighs to return to the standing position.

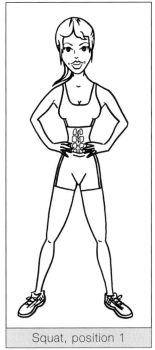

Squat, position 1

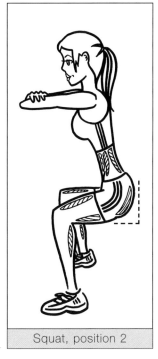

Squat, position 2

WEEK TWO, DAY THREE
MyoKinetics reverse lunge

You may be a little tender today after yesterday's squats, so make sure that you execute your lunges slowly and don't skimp on the stretch! Kneel on the floor. Lift your right leg and plant your right foot on the floor in front of you. To facilitate a stretch and prime the muscles, place your hands on your right thigh and, keeping your familiarisation exercises in mind, gently lunge your weight forward. Keeping your hips angled forward, you should feel the stretch in your glutes, hamstrings and surrounding muscles. Hold for 15 seconds.

From this kneeling position, raise your left knee approximately 10 cm off the floor. Remind yourself of your core stability and your breathing technique as you hold this position of sustained tension for a count of five seconds. Pushing through your right heel, gradually straighten your legs (don't lock your knees) through a five-second count to a split stance. Immediately begin to reverse this movement through a five-second count to the starting position just before your knee touches the floor. One full repetition must take 15 seconds to complete. Complete three consecutive repetitions on this leg, followed by three repetitions on the opposite leg. Practise these sets twice more throughout the day.

Always stretch before you proceed with a lunge

Lunge, position 1

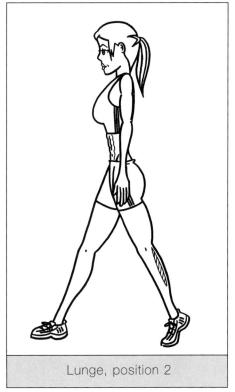

Lunge, position 2

WEEK TWO, DAY FOUR
MyoKinetics tricep dips

As the triceps work to assist in most upper body exercises, this area is already primed and stretched before we begin. The following movement utilises only a short range to achieve the sustained tension, thereby reducing the risk of joint strain. In a seated position on the floor, bend your knees and place the soles of both feet on the floor. Place your hands flat on the floor, fingers facing forward, behind your hips. In this position, your arms are straight and in a slight lean back, your shoulders are directly over your hands. Set your core stability, lock in your shoulder blades and be conscious of your breathing as you lift your bottom off the floor, transferring your weight onto both hands. This is the starting position. Slowly bend your elbows and lower your body towards the ground. Just before your bottom touches the floor, hold this position of sustained tension for a five-second count then press yourself back to the starting position. Take care not to jerk this movement and, although your arms should be straight, try not to lock them, which would increase joint stress.

Complete three consecutive repetitions and practise this set twice more throughout the day.

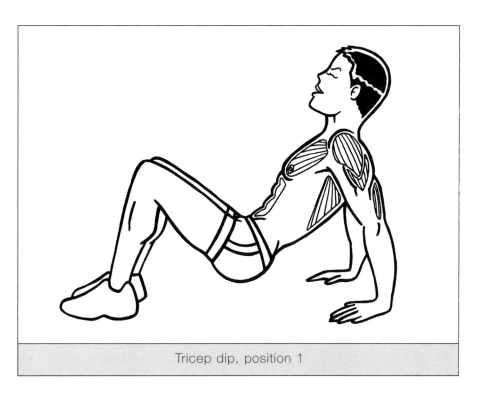

Tricep dip, position 1

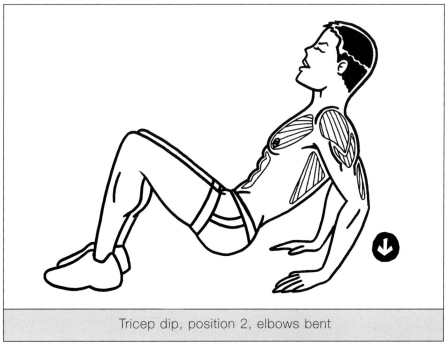

Tricep dip, position 2, elbows bent

WEEK TWO, DAY FIVE
MyoKinetics 'ab trio'

You may curse me while you're doing these, but I promise you'll thank me later! This really is a complete workout for your mid-section, from every angle.

It is very important that you revise the familiarisation task before attempting this trio. Your core stability is essential for optimum deep tissue intensity, so limber up that navel area and let's give it a shot.

Lie on your back on the floor, knees bent (heels close to your bottom) and arms stretched laterally, palms down. Set your core stability, remember your breathing and keep both shoulders 'pinned' to the floor throughout the rotations. The first of the trio involves a rotation to either side to target the obliques. Your upper body will remain locked in its current position and the movement will be a pivot from the waist. The degree of rotation achieved will depend on your strength, as well as joint and muscle flexibility. It's not a competition, so don't overdo it!

Ab trio, position 1

1. In the starting position, lift your feet off the floor and lock yourself into the 45-degree hip angle, as indicated in the illustration. Through a five-second count, gradually rotate your hips and legs to one side, hold the position of sustained tension (knees are not to touch the floor!) for a five-second count. Through a further five-second count, focus on pushing your lower back into the floor to pull yourself back to the centre starting position. Repeat this on the opposite side.

Ab trio, position 2

2. Maintain the central starting position and slide your arms in by your sides, palms down. Applying your familiarisation skills to a reverse crunch, roll your vertebrae one at a time, starting from your coccyx (tailbone). This is only a short-range movement intended to gently lift your bottom off the floor, again through a five-second count. Hold for a further five-second count (remember to breathe!) and lower through a five-second count back to the starting position.

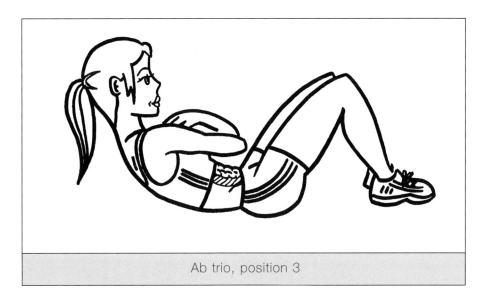

Ab trio, position 3

3. From the central starting position return the soles of your feet to the floor and, through a five-second count, begin to roll each vertebra off the floor, starting from your neck. At full contraction, hold the sustained tension for a count of five. Return to the starting position through a further five-second count.

Repeat this trio three consecutive times and practise the full set twice more throughout the day.

WEEK TWO, DAY SIX
MyoKinetics bridge and tuck

This is a compound movement that will really put your core stability skills to the test. Working and stretching the glutes, hamstrings, abs and upper body, this movement uses your shoulder joint as the 'pendulum'. You will find it combined with other exercises when you come to the workout combinations in week three. As it incorporates stretching, no specific stretch is necessary prior to commencing.

In a seated position on the floor, with your legs outstretched in front of you, place your hands flat on the floor. They should be just in front of your hips, with your fingers pointed forwards. With your posture and breathing in mind, set your core stability by drawing your navel back towards your spine. Shift your weight onto your hands and lift your bottom off the floor into the starting position. Through a count of no less than five seconds, shift your weight forward. The first position of sustained tension is in the bridge position. As you hold this position for a count of five seconds, you will feel a stretch through your shoulders, chest and thighs. You will feel sustained tension in your glutes and supporting upper body muscles, and in your abdominal area. Gradually reverse this movement through another five-second count, lowering your torso back through to the starting position. You must 'tuck' your abdominal muscles in tight to allow you to pull your hips through your arms and back to the starting position. You must finish with your bottom behind your hand placement. As soon as you reach this position, start your second repetition immediately without lowering your bottom to the floor. Complete three consecutive repetitions and practise this set twice more throughout the day.

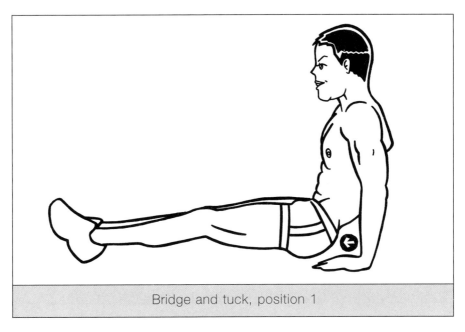

Bridge and tuck, position 1

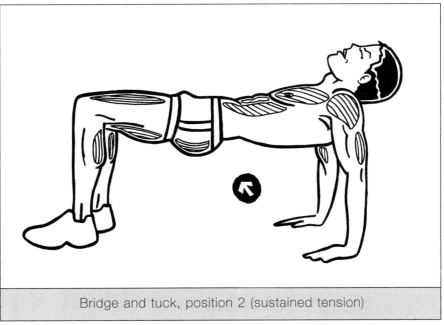

Bridge and tuck, position 2 (sustained tension)

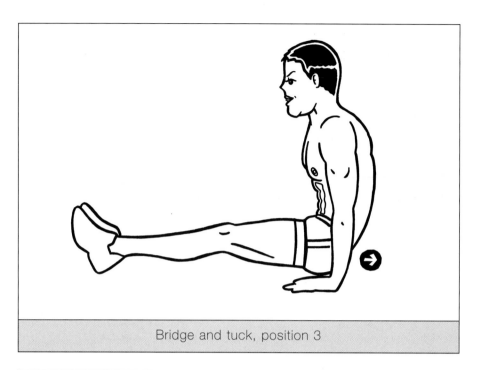

Bridge and tuck, position 3

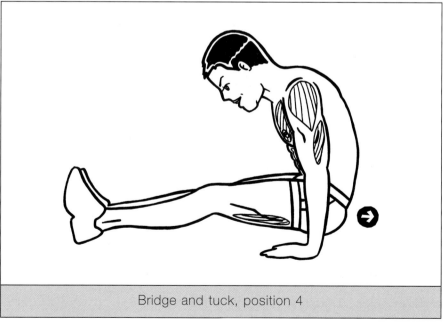

Bridge and tuck, position 4

WEEK TWO, DAY SEVEN
MyoKinetics **skaters squat**

This is a compound movement, which involves several muscle groups, but the glute is the main focus of your mind-muscle connection. You may have observed (I have!) that professionals in skating sports commonly boast cute little bubble butts – we can all learn from their methods. Trust me, one workout with the following exercise and you'll be a skaters squat devotee for life!

To stretch the muscle group before commencing, perform the kneeling lunge stretch (page 85) on each leg. Until you perfect your balance and technique, you may require some assistance with your balance in the form of a chair back, positioned approximately a metre in front you. In a standing position with your feet together, set your core stability by drawing your navel back towards your spine. Remind yourself of correct posture and breathing throughout the movement. There should be a slight bend in your right leg as you begin to raise it behind you, with your toes pointed towards the floor at all times (see illustration overleaf). Like a pendulum, your upper body will simultaneously tilt forward from the hip joint, keeping your back 'flat' and your arms outstretched in front of you (like Superman in full flight). At this point, hold onto your chair back for balance if necessary. A five-second count will take you to the goal position where your right leg is stretched out behind you, close to parallel with the floor, and your left leg is in a semi-squat position, supporting your body weight (see illustration overleaf). Hold this position of sustained tension for a five-second count and gradually reverse the movement, using a five-second count to return to the starting position. Complete three consecutive repetitions on this leg, followed by three repetitions on the other leg. Practise this set twice more throughout the day.

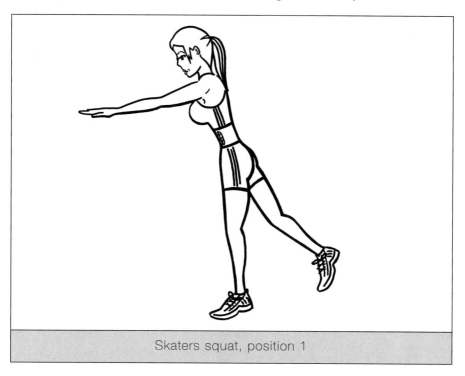

Skaters squat, position 1

Skaters squat, position 2

chapter eight
Week three: pulling it all together

Progressive levels of intensity

The following *MyoKinetics* workouts are divided into three levels:

   Level 1 is the *beginner* level

   Level 2 is the *intermediate* level

   Level 3 is the *advanced* level

Cardiovascular levels

There are also three progressive levels of cardiovascular exercise (CV), to be performed on alternate days to your workouts.

➋   CV1 indicates a 20-minute walk at a 'comfortable' speed of approximately 4-5 km/h (depending on your fitness level).

➋   CV2 indicates a 20-minute walk, increasing the intensity by speed (5-6 km/h), rather than time.

❷   CV3 indicates a 20-minute walk, increasing the speed once again to a very brisk 7-8 km/h.

How should you progress?

I want to make it crystal clear that it is not necessary for you to reach optimum intensity in any given time frame, if at all. If you are a novice to exercise and you feel that you are reaping significant benefits from level one, then by all means, stay at this level for as long as you please. If your goal is to apply your *MyoKinetics* skills to your existing gym workout, then you have a choice. You can begin the following regime in preparation for your workout or you can simply head straight into your existing regime and apply your *MyoKinetics* techniques. Whatever your goal, your progress depends on your physical capabilities. The most important factor is to ensure an ever-growing awareness of the mind-muscle connection that is the foundation of *MyoKinetics*. Don't be tempted to challenge yourself to complete your workout faster than is indicated, or to progress to a higher level of intensity too quickly. It's OK for you to be overconfident but your body may not share your enthusiasm! Ultimately, you could risk self-defeat by losing your focus on form and technique, as well as overtraining and risking injury. If you do choose the gradual progression to the advanced level, you will certainly have reached peak fitness and will be well on your way to achieving optimum deep tissue toning. Personally, I have never felt the need to increase the intensity past level three. If you feel that it is becoming 'easy' to complete, then it is highly likely that your mind-muscle skills could be flagging, allowing 'helper' muscles to pitch in. In this situation, may I suggest that you go back to the beginning of the book and allow yourself to practise and reinforce the basic principles.

Fairytale: *The more you sweat, the more body fat you are losing …*

Fact: How many times have you seen exercise enthusiasts enduring their workouts in a tortuous (not to mention embarrassing) 'sweat' suit. The first time I witnessed this was about 20 years ago. I'll never forget it. A woman would jog past my house religiously each morning wearing about four woolly jumpers and a pair of towelling track pants lined with a garbage bag, to encourage profuse sweating. What a nut! Unfortunately, I still see this sort of behaviour every now and then. Perhaps it gives the plastic-clad fanatic a false impression of a high-intensity workout. As it is usually a woman's thighs that receive the 'plastic wrap' treatment, I'm guessing that the intent is to 'spot reduce'. The fact is that one would risk severe dehydration, which brings with it fatigue and the risk of serious side-effects, such as muscle cramps, mineral imbalances, and headache and nausea, not to mention the intense stress of it all! If you have lost any 'weight' from perspiring, it will be predominantly water, which is regained as soon as you have a swig from your water bottle. If anything, you are actually hindering fat loss. That's right, the less clothing worn, the better. Our body has to maintain a core temperature, so the more heat we lose to the atmosphere when exercising, the more calories burned. Now, before you whip off the bin-liners and power walk in your birthday suit, try finding yourself a happy medium! The bottom line? Perspiration is only water, not fat. It is a self-protection mechanism that your body employs to prevent over-heating. You can't melt or sweat-out fat!

The most effective, time-efficient fat burning methods to complement *MyoKinetics* for optimum fitness, definition and tone

Walk this way

Walking is one of the best all-round cardiovascular activities. It's inexpensive – all you need is a comfy pair of shoes. It can be performed by anybody of any fitness level and can be easily incorporated into your daily routine. Whether used as a source of relaxation or a means of transport, a brisk 20-30 minutes each day will do wonders for your health, while generating significant fat burning benefits. The amount of calories you burn can vary significantly and will be dictated by speed, intensity and terrain. Walking is included in the *MyoKinetics* weekly planner outlined in later chapters. For the sake of consistency and time-efficiency, I suggest that you increase the intensity rather than the duration, as your fitness level rises.

Although brisk walking is perfectly sufficient, you may wish to incorporate some interval training, such as short bursts of jogging or sprinting for variety. For example, walk for a minute, jog for a minute; or walk for two minutes and sprint for 30 seconds. Of course, your cardiovascular fitness will determine the duration of each 'burst', but it is a great way of increasing your cardio intensity, without having to surrender hours of your precious time.

Jump to it!

The skipping rope is certainly one of my favourites. Not only is it time-efficient, it provides a pretty intense workout, burning a whopping 10-15 calories per minute. Your last memory of skipping may be in the playground at primary school. Remember? Most of us would skip at every opportunity. It was never considered exercise back then – it was simply a fun way to pass the time. My … how things have changed! If it has been a while, you may get a rude shock when you pick up that rope again. There's no denying it's tough work. It's important to start off slowly and gradually increase the duration and intensity as your fitness level progresses. Don't be disheartened if you find yourself out of breath after 30 seconds. You'll be surprised at how quickly you and your rope become reacquainted. So, what are some of the 'perks' of skipping?

- Unparalleled, time-efficient and inexpensive calorie-burning
- Improved cardiovascular fitness
- Increased speed and power
- Enhanced balance and coordination
- Strengthened muscles and bones.

Skipping ropes come in a range of lengths and materials, so the first thing you need to do is purchase one that is the appropriate length and the easiest to use. As you may be incorporating skipping into your *MyoKinetics* workout regime, heavy leather ropes or those with features such as weighted handles are not necessary. I recommend a light plastic rope, durable and inexpensive. There is a very simple rule of thumb to choose the appropriate length: hold both handles and allow the rope to hang by your side. Stand on the rope and both handles should just reach your armpit.

Getting started . . .

You will need a good pair of shoes. Those designed for cross-training or aerobics are ideal. For the girls … a good sports bra is essential. Try to avoid concrete surfaces. Wooden, rubber or carpeted floors are best. If you are skipping indoors, make sure that 'Fido' is safely in his kennel and that you don't take out the overhead light fittings!

Now for a few golden rules and you're ready to go …

- ➔ Before starting, gently stretch your calf muscles by standing on the balls of your feet on the edge of a step or curb. A five-minute pre-skipping walk to warm up your muscles is ideal.

- ➔ Keep your jumps low to the ground. Proficient skipping doesn't require vigorous movements.

- ➔ Keep your knees 'soft' and use your calf muscles.

- ➔ Turn the rope by flipping your wrists, limiting upper arm involvement. Keep your elbows close to your body and your hands down by your sides.

- ➔ Land softly and gently. Pretend that the floor is quite fragile and that you'll break it if you land heavily.

- ➔ Breathe!

Warm up

Although it is not essential to do a specific warm up prior to commencing the *MyoKinetics* workouts, I certainly recommend it if time permits. Even a brisk five- or ten-minute walk around the block would suffice. If you do choose to progress to the advanced level (three), including higher impact moves such as skipping and plyometrics (explosive movements), then a five- to ten-minute warm-up walk becomes essential.

By the way, if you are one of those impatient individuals who has just flicked to the workout section in an attempt to bypass the detail … you've been sprung! You are only cheating yourself out of results. Go back to the beginning and I'll meet you back here when you've done your homework!

In this section you will find three *MyoKinetics* workouts, each comprising four exercise units. The three levels are dictated by specific repetitions, technique variations and timing. Regardless of your current fitness level, I suggest that for the first week you start at level one to enable optimum focus on your skills. The three workouts have been designed to be rotated, to encourage a holistic regime. Ideally, you would perform each workout once a week (i.e. Monday: workout one, Wednesday: workout two, Friday: workout three). Workout three incorporates a technique known as 'plyometrics' and is very taxing on your body, so I think you'll find once a week is sufficient. Breaks between sets are not to exceed one minute. These are short, intense workouts designed to achieve the maximum result from the minimum time commitment.

A note to beginners

If you are a complete novice to exercise and you are happy familiarising yourself with one of the workouts for a few weeks, this is perfectly acceptable. The optimum timing of each move in the exercises is five seconds. If at first you feel this is too difficult, you may need to reduce your count and gradually build up to five seconds. The same rule applies if you require more time to complete each set. Workout three is slightly more difficult than workouts one and two due to the plyometric component, so if you find workouts one and two difficult, I suggest that you postpone the inclusion of workout three for a few weeks until you build your strength and fitness levels.

WORKOUT ONE

TOTAL TIME COMMITMENT:

Level 1: Beginners – 18 minutes

Level 2: Intermediate – 23 minutes

Level 3: Advanced – 33 minutes

All repetitions should be performed consecutively, without periods of rest in between. Ensure that you have no longer than one minute delay between each exercise.

I have not given generous explanations of *MyoKinetics* techniques in this section. If you have completed your familiarisation tasks conscientiously you should now be well enough acquainted with your mind-muscle technique, core stability, posture and breathing techniques to apply them to these movements automatically.

EXERCISE 1
MyoKinetics squat / lunge
LEVELS 1 - 3

EXERCISE 1
MyoKinetics squat / lunge

In a standing position, step one foot out to the side to form a wide stance. Use your 3 x 5-second count technique to complete the full movement and sustain tension. Perform three consecutive repetitions and, without pause, step your feet back together in preparation for the lunge. Step your right leg back and kneel into the starting position of the reverse lunge. Complete your level of consecutive repetitions on each leg.

➡ preparation: hold this stretch for 15-20 seconds

Level 1

Complete 1 set of 4 repetitions of squats, followed by 1 set of 4 repetitions of lunges on each leg = 12 repetitions.

1 set of 4 repetitions of squats

1 set of 4 repetitions of lunges on each leg

Maximum time allowance to complete the set: **3.5 minutes**

Level 2

Complete 1 set of 4 repetitions of squats and 1 set of 4 repetitions of lunges on each leg.

1 set of 4 repetitions of squats

1 set of 4 repetitions of lunges on each leg

REPEAT

Maximum time allowance to complete the set: **6 minutes**

Level 3

➤ Complete 1 set of 6 repetitions of squats followed immediately by 1 minute of skipping rope

➤ Complete 1 set of 6 repetitions of lunges (right) followed immediately by 1 minute of skipping rope

➤ Complete 1 set of 6 repetitions of lunges (left) followed immediately by 1 minute of skipping rope

Total = 18 repetitions and 3 minutes of skipping rope

1 set of 6 repetitions of squats

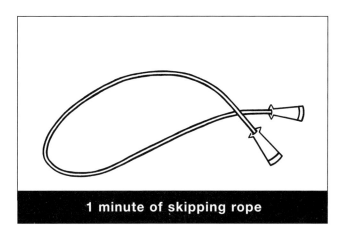

1 minute of skipping rope

1 set of 6 repetitions of lunges on right leg

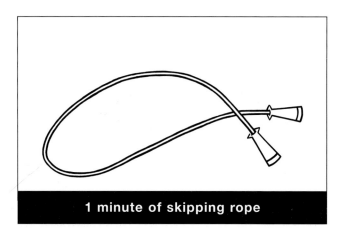

1 minute of skipping rope

1 set of 6 repetitions of lunges on left leg

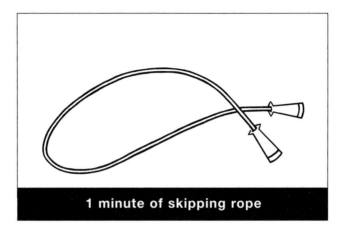

1 minute of skipping rope

Maximum time allowance to complete the set: **8 minutes**

EXERCISE 2
MyoKinetics push-up and burpee
LEVELS 1 - 3

EXERCISE 2
MyoKinetics push-up and burpee

Assume the push-up position with your hands positioned just wide of your shoulders and your arms straight. Complete your first repetition lowering your torso to the floor through a five-second count until you reach the position of sustained tension (chest just clear of the floor). Hold for a five-second count before returning to the starting position. To complete your burpee raise your knees off the floor and with an explosive movement, bend your knees as you jump with both feet, bringing your knees in to your chest and immediately jumping back into the starting position (see illustrations on pages 118 and 119).

Your hands remain in the correct position for push-ups, so you are now ready to go straight into your next push-up repetition. Continue this alternate push-up and burpee duo until you have completed your level of consecutive repetitions.

➔ preparation: hold this stretch for 20-30 seconds

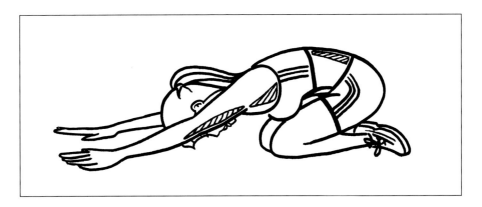

Level 1

Complete 1 set of 4 repetitions of push-ups, alternating each repetition with a burpee.

Total = 4 repetitions of push-ups and 4 burpees

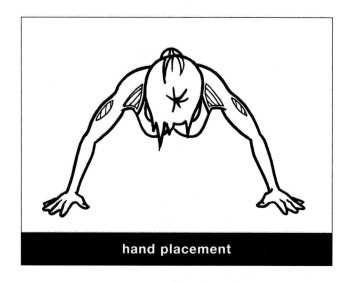

hand placement

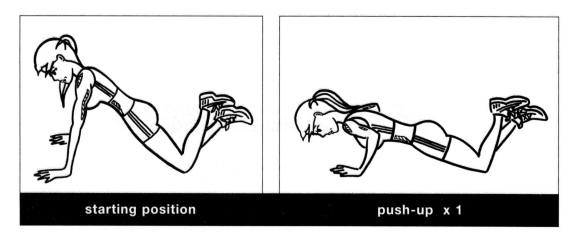

starting position

push-up x 1

burpee x 1

REPEAT 3 TIMES

Maximum time allowance to complete the set: **3 minutes**

Level 2

Complete 1 set of 8 repetitions of push-ups, alternating each repetition with a burpee.

Total = 8 repetitions of push-ups and 8 burpees

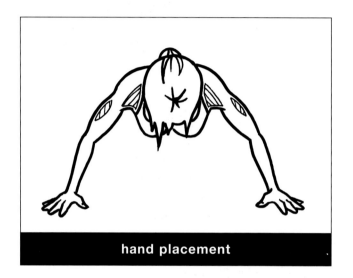

hand placement

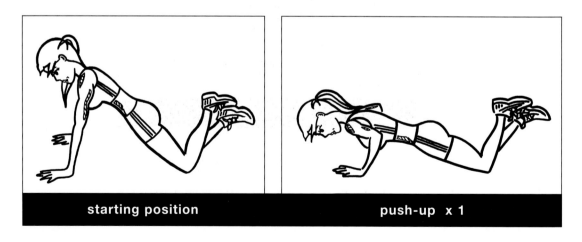

starting position

push-up x 1

burpee x 1

REPEAT 7 TIMES

Maximum time allowance to complete the set: **4 minutes**

Level 3

Complete 2 sets of 5 repetitions in the advanced push-up position (on your toes), alternating each repetition with a burpee and 30 seconds of skipping between each set.

Total = 10 repetitions of push-ups, 10 burpees and 1 minute of skipping

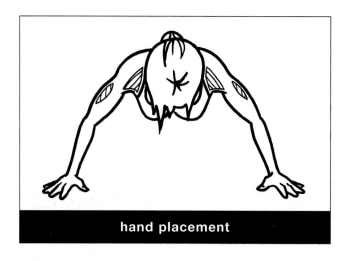

hand placement

advanced push-up x 1

burpee x 1

REPEAT 4 TIMES

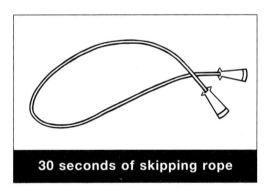

30 seconds of skipping rope

REPEAT THIS ENTIRE COMBINATION
TO COMPLETE TWO FULL SETS

Maximum time allowance to complete the set: **4 minutes**

EXERCISE 3
MyoKinetics bridge and tuck
LEVELS 1 - 3

EXERCISE 3
MyoKinetics bridge and tuck

The bridge and tuck (see pages 93, 94) combined is considered one complete repetition.

➡ preparation: hold this stretch for 20 seconds

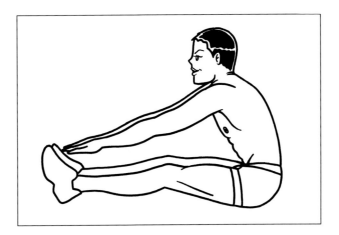

Level 1

Complete 1 set of 6 repetitions, alternating each full repetition with the 15-second hamstring stretch.

Total = 6 repetitions and 6 x 15 second stretches

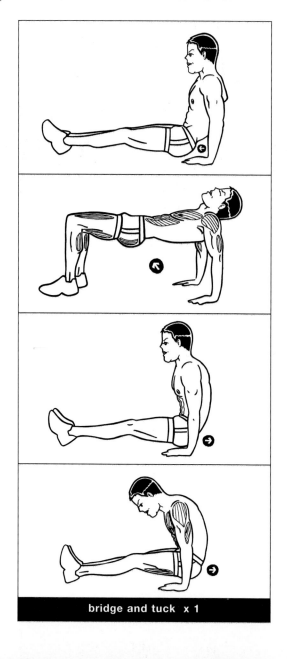

bridge and tuck x 1

stretch for 15 seconds

REPEAT 5 TIMES

Maximum time allowance to complete the set: **4 minutes**

Level 2

Complete 2 sets of 6 repetitions, alternating each set with the 15-second hamstring stretch.

Total = 12 repetitions and 2 x 15 second stretches

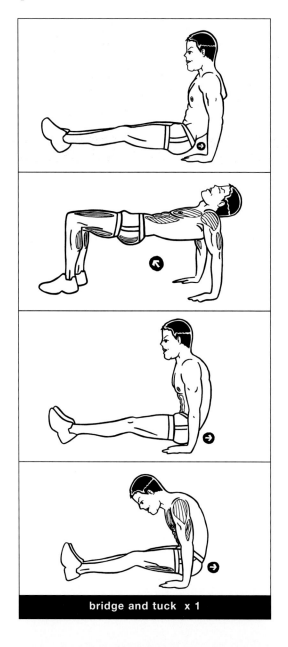

bridge and tuck x 1

stretch for 15 seconds

REPEAT

Maximum time allowance to complete the set: **4 minutes**

Level 3

Complete 2 sets of 6 repetitions, alternating each set with the 15-second hamstring stretch and 1 minute of skipping.

Total = 12 repetitions, 2 x 15 second stretches and 2 minutes of skipping

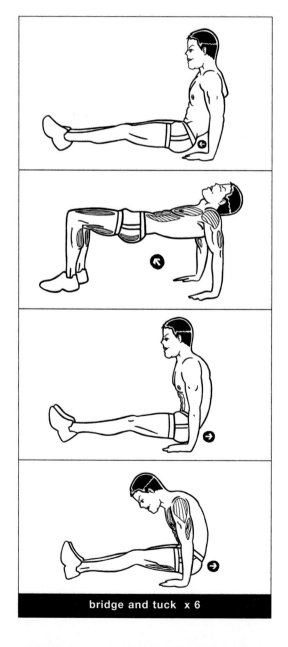

bridge and tuck x 6

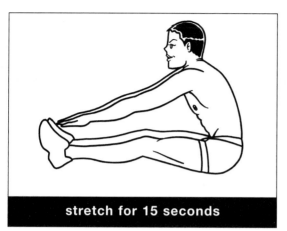

stretch for 15 seconds

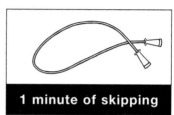

1 minute of skipping

REPEAT

Maximum time allowance to complete the set: **6 minutes**

EXERCISE 4
MyoKinetics ab trio
LEVELS 1 - 3

EXERCISE 4
MyoKinetics ab trio

The consecutive performance of these three ab exercises combined is considered one complete repetition.

➔   preparation: hold this stretch for 15 seconds on each side

Level 1

Complete 1 set of 5 repetitions of the following combination: rotation left, rotation right, reverse crunch and crunch, each held for a 5-second count at the sustained tension position.

Total = 5 full repetitions

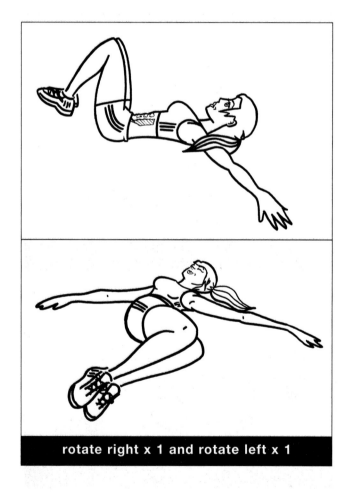

rotate right x 1 and rotate left x 1

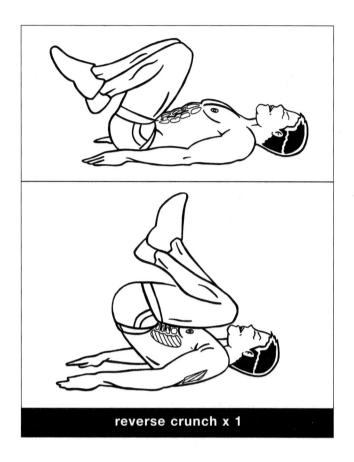

reverse crunch x 1

crunch x 1

REPEAT 4 TIMES

Maximum time allowance to complete the set: **4.5 minutes**

Level 2

Complete 1 set of 8 repetitions of the same combination.

Total = 8 repetitions

rotate right x 1 and rotate left x 1

reverse crunch x 1

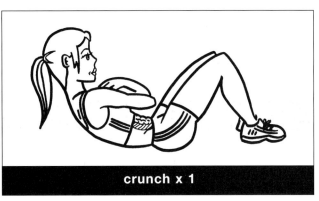

crunch x 1

REPEAT 7 TIMES

Maximum time allowance to complete the set: **6 minutes**

Level 3

Complete 2 sets of 6 repetitions of the same combination, but straighten legs on the side rotations and reverse crunch (see illustrations). Alternate each set with 30 seconds of intense skipping.

Total = 12 repetitions and 1 minute of skipping

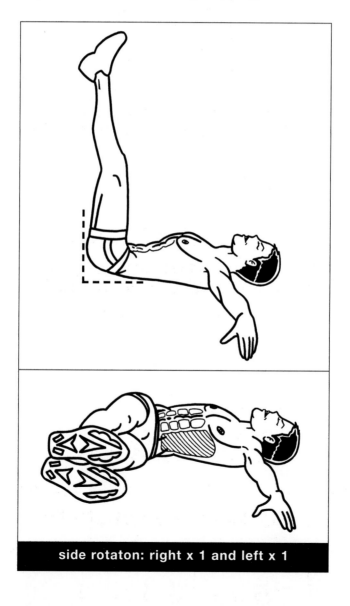

side rotaton: right x 1 and left x 1

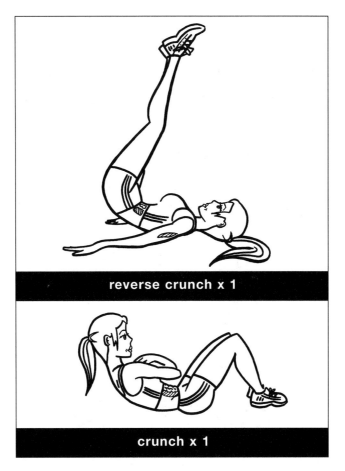

reverse crunch x 1

crunch x 1

REPEAT 5 TIMES

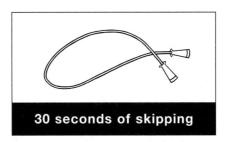

30 seconds of skipping

REPEAT THIS ENTIRE COMBINATION
TO COMPLETE 2 FULL SETS

Maximum time allowance to complete the set: **10 minutes**

WORKOUT TWO

TOTAL TIME COMMITMENT:

Level 1: beginners – 18 minutes

Level 2: intermediate – 22 minutes

Level 3: advanced – 32 minutes

EXERCISE 1
MyoKinetics skaters squat and rear lunge

This 'dynamic duo' is not only a great butt blaster, but it will certainly raise your heart rate a beat or two!

You'll be familiar with the skaters squat from last week's practice, but the rear lunge is a slight variation on the reverse lunge.

Complete the appropriate level of consecutive repetitions of the skaters squat on one leg and continue, without pause, on the other leg, finishing with both feet together in an upright position. To execute the rear lunge, remember your breathing and posture as you take a deep step back with your right leg. Bend your left knee, lowering your right knee (to a count of five) towards the floor. As you descend, gradually raise your arms laterally to perform a 'side-delt raise'. This action also aids stability and balance. Remember your mind-muscle connection as you hold the position of sustained tension for a five-second count. Push through your left heel and lift your body through a five-second count back to a standing position, gradually lowering your arms back to your sides as you ascend. Repeat all repetitions on one leg before changing to the other.

→ preparation: hold this stretch for 15 seconds on each leg

Level 1

Complete 1 set of 3 repetitions (on each leg) of the skaters squat, followed immediately by 3 repetitions (on each leg) of the rear lunge.

Total = 12 repetitions

skaters squat: right x 3 and left x 3

rear lunge: right x 3 and left x 3

Maximum time to complete the set: **4 minutes**

Level 2

Complete 1 set of 3 repetitions (on each leg) of the skaters squat, followed immediately by 3 repetitions (on each leg) of the rear lunge. Repeat.

Total = 24 repetitions

skaters squat: right x 3 and left x 3

rear lunge: right x 3 and left x 3

REPEAT

Maximum time allowance to complete the set: **6 minutes**

Level 3

Complete 1 set of 6 repetitions (on each leg) of the skaters squat. Without pause, skip rope for 1 minute and continue with 1 set of 6 repetitions (on each leg) of lunges, followed by a second set of skipping for 1 minute.

Total: 24 repetitions and 2 minutes of skipping

skaters squat: x 6 right and x 6 left

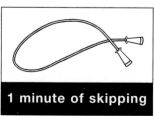

1 minute of skipping

rear lunge: x 6 right and x 6 left

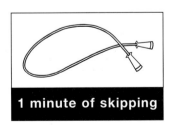

1 minute of skipping

Maximum time allowance to complete the set: **8 minutes**

EXERCISE 2
MyoKinetics three-point crunch

The three-point crunch provides a great ab workout from every angle. Using the same technique as the basic ab crunch, lie on your back, knees bent and slightly apart. Extend both arms in front of you, hands together. Through a five-second count, remember to roll each vertebra off the floor, reaching your hands through the centre of your legs. Hold this point of sustained tension for a five-second count and slowly return to the starting position through a further five-second count. Repeat this movement reaching your hands to one side of your legs (using the same five-second count) to create a slight rotation, and again to the opposite side. The three-point crunch consists of a centre-right-left action, with five-second holds at each point of sustained tension. There should be no pauses and each trio completes one repetition.

➲   preparation : hold this stretch for 15 seconds each side

Level 1

Complete 1 set of 4 repetitions.

Total = 4 repetitions

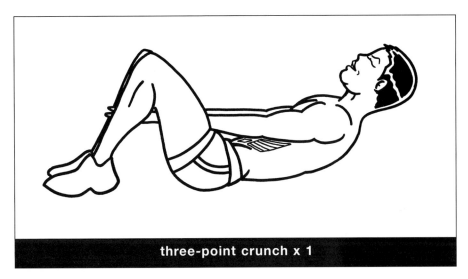

three-point crunch x 1

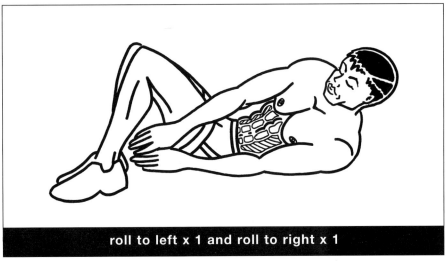

roll to left x 1 and roll to right x 1

REPEAT 3 TIMES

Maximum time allowance to complete the set: **3.5 minutes**

Level 2

Complete 1 set of 6 repetitions.

Total = 6 repetitions

three-point crunch x 1

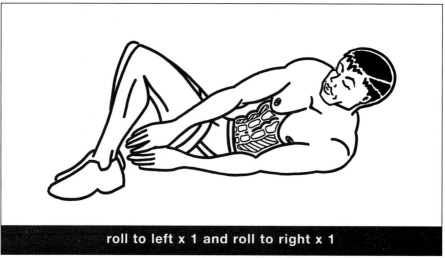

roll to left x 1 and roll to right x 1

REPEAT 5 TIMES

Maximum time allowance to complete the set: **4.5 minutes**

Level 3

Complete 1 set of 10 repetitions.

Total = 10 repetitions

three-point crunch x 1

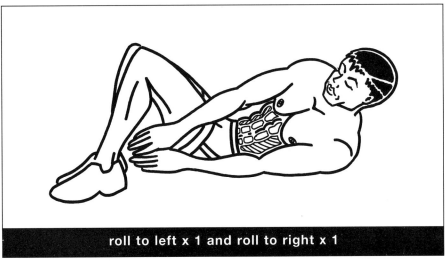

roll to left x 1 and roll to right x 1

REPEAT 9 TIMES

Maximum time allowance to complete the set: **7.5 minutes**

EXERCISE 3
MyoKinetics bridge and tuck
LEVELS 1 - 3

EXERCISE 3
MyoKinetics bridge and tuck

The bridge and tuck (see pages 93, 94) combined is considered one complete repetition.

➔   preparation: hold this stretch for 20 seconds

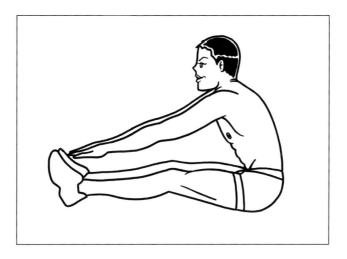

Level 1

Complete 1 set of 6 repetitions, alternating each full repetition with the 15-second hamstring stretch.

Total = 6 repetitions and 6 x 15 second stretches

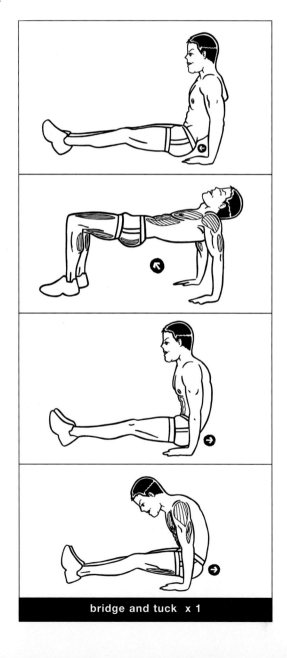

bridge and tuck x 1

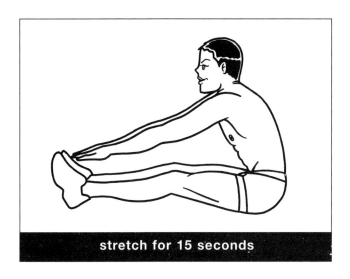

stretch for 15 seconds

REPEAT 5 TIMES

Maximum time allowance to complete the set: **4 minutes**

Level 2

Complete 2 sets of 6 repetitions, alternating each *set* with the 15-second hamstring stretch.

Total = 12 repetitions and 2 x 15 second stretches

bridge and tuck x 6

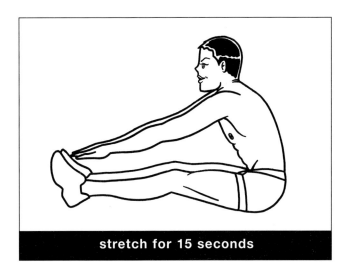

stretch for 15 seconds

REPEAT 11 TIMES

Maximum time allowance to complete the set: **4 minutes**

Level 3

Complete 2 sets of 6 repetitions, alternating each set with the 15-second hamstring stretch and 1 minute of skipping.

Total = 12 repetitions, 2 x 15 second stretches and 2 minutes of skipping

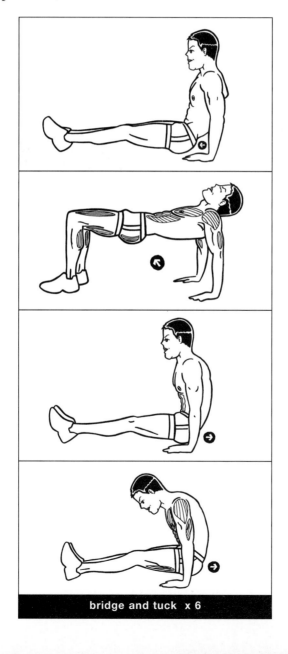

bridge and tuck x 6

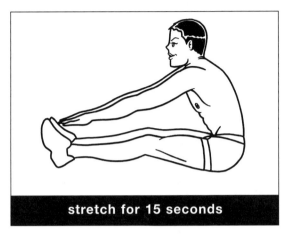

stretch for 15 seconds

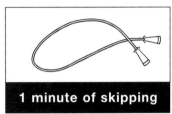

1 minute of skipping

REPEAT

Maximum time allowance to complete the set: **6 minutes**

EXERCISE 4

MyoKinetics tricep press and cat stretch

LEVELS 1 - 3

EXERCISE 4
MyoKinetics tricep press and cat stretch

The range of movement and the body positioning of this exercise are similar to those of the basic push-up. Although this is considered a compound movement, we will change the focus of the primary muscle from the chest to the triceps ... here's how.

Observe the narrow hand placement beneath the chest (as opposed to parallel with the shoulders for regular push-ups). Follow the same principles for posture, core stability and breathing as you would for push-ups, but keep your elbows in close to your body (pointing towards your feet). Begin at the lowered position of sustained tension with your chest just off the floor for a five-second count. Focusing on your tricep muscles, count through a further five seconds as you push your torso away from the floor until your arms are straight. Lower for a count of five seconds until you reach the starting position. To give your triceps a well-earned break, at the end of each set push your bottom back towards your heels for a 15-second cat stretch, returning to the starting position to continue until you have completed the exercise.

➔   preparation: hold this stretch for 20-30 seconds

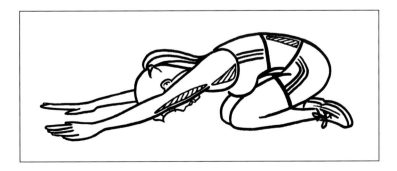

Level 1

Complete 2 sets of 4 repetitions, alternating each set with the 15-second cat stretch.

Total = 8 repetitions and 2 x 15 second stretches

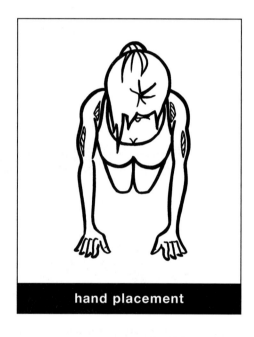

hand placement

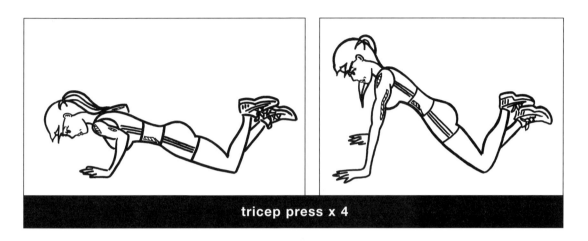

tricep press x 4

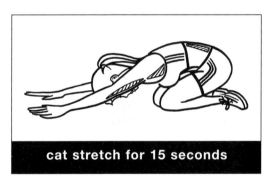

cat stretch for 15 seconds

REPEAT

Maximum time allowance to complete the set: **3.5 minutes**

Level 2

Complete 2 sets of 8 repetitions, alternating each set with the 15-second stretch.

Total = 16 repetitions and 2 x 15 second stretches

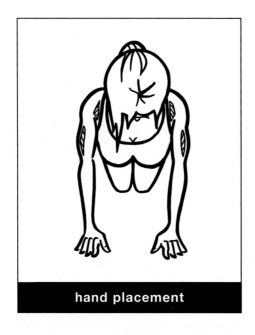

hand placement

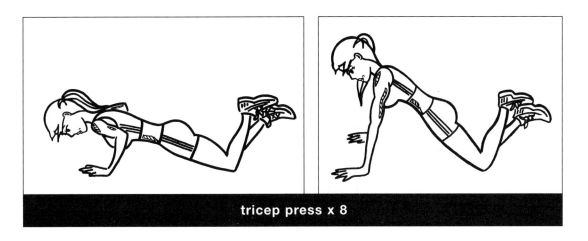

tricep press x 8

cat stretch for 15 seconds

REPEAT

Maximum time allowance to complete the set: **4.5 minutes**

Level 3

Complete 2 sets of 8 repetitions in the advanced position (on your toes as opposed to your knees), alternating each set with the 15-second stretch and 1 minute of skipping.

Total = 16 repetitions, 2 x 15 second stretches and 2 minutes of skipping

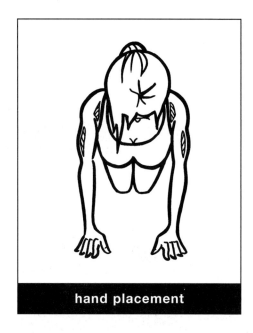

hand placement

tricep press x 8

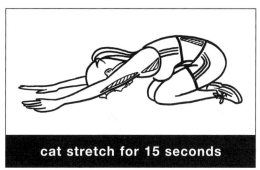

cat stretch for 15 seconds

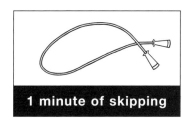

1 minute of skipping

REPEAT

Maximum time allowance to complete the set: **7.5 minutes**

WORKOUT THREE

TOTAL TIME COMMITMENT:

Level 1: beginners – 17 minutes

Level 2: intermediate – 24 minutes

Level 3: advanced – 33.5 minutes

I have incorporated a technique known as plyometrics in the following workout. Plyometrics helps us to develop a further element of 'explosive' strength, but it often increases the intensity of a given movement, so pace yourself. As always, be aware of your mind-muscle connection, posture, core stability and breathing throughout all movements. The two exercises using plyometrics in this workout are squats and push-ups. Before you begin this workout, we're going to go through a couple of tasks to familiarise you with this technique, as well as prepare your muscles.

Task 1

To reduce any impact on your joints, bend your knees and practise rising up onto your toes and returning your heels to the floor. Repeat this 10 times. Now perform the same movement, but as your heels rise, add a little jump, landing back on the balls of your feet, allowing your heels to smoothly roll back to the floor. In your mind, try to make the tips of your toes the last thing to leave the floor and the first thing to make contact with it on your descent. Always keep a bend in your knees. This action can also be practised to reduce the impact of skipping.

Task 2

On your knees and in the push-up position (with your arms out-stretched), bend your elbows to lower your body 10 centimetres or so, and as you push away from the floor create a more explosive action to lift both hands a few centimetres off the floor. As your hands land, it is important to keep your elbows bent to reduce the impact on your joints. Keep this short movement going for a few repetitions until you develop a smooth, continuous action.

EXERCISE 1
MyoKinetics plyometric squat
LEVELS 1 - 3

EXERCISE 1
MyoKinetics plyometric squat

This exercise is the same as the basic squat, with the exception of a more *explosive* ascent. Standing with your feet positioned about 15 centimetres wider than each shoulder, cross your arms in front of your chest (that 'Jeannie thing' again). Remember to set your core stability and posture as you bend your knees and hips and, through a five-second count, lower your bottom towards the floor. When your thighs are parallel with the floor, hold this position of sustained tension for a further five-second count. From this position, disregard the usual five-second return to the standing position. Instead, you will need to muster an 'explosive' action as you rise, enabling a 'jump' before you return to the starting position. NEVER land without a bend in your knees! The movement should be very smooth, allowing you to continue without pause into the next repetition.

➜ preparation: hold this stretch for 15-20 seconds

Level 1

Complete 2 sets of 5 repetitions. Between each set, hold the basic stretch position (see illustration) for a 15-second count.

Total = 10 repetitions and 2 x 15 second stretches

plyometric squat x 5

stretch for 15 seconds

REPEAT

Maximum time allowance to complete the set: **3 minutes**

Level 2

Complete 2 sets of 8 repetitions. Between each set, hold the basic stretch position for a 15-second count.

Total = 16 repetitions and 2 x 15-second stretches

plyometric squat x 8

Maximum time allowance to complete the set: **4.5 minutes**

stretch for 15 seconds

REPEAT

Maximum time allowance to complete the set: **4.5 minutes**

Level 3

Complete 2 sets of 10 repetitions. Between each set, hold the basic stretch position for a 15-second count, followed by 1 minute of skipping.

Total = 20 repetitions, 2 x 15-second stretches and 2 minutes of skipping

plyometric squat x 10

stretch for 15 seconds

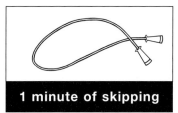

1 minute of skipping

REPEAT

Maximum time allowance to complete the set: **7.5 minutes**

EXERCISE 2
MyoKinetics ab 'squeeze and crunch'

This is a variation of the basic crunch providing a deep ab workout. You will feel this strengthen your pelvic floor muscles and fatigue your inner thighs and hip flexor muscles, which often results in relief of some lower back stiffness.

Lie on the floor with your knees bent, feet flat on the floor, your heels close to your bottom, and position a rolled up towel, or a cushion between your knees. Focus on pulling your navel towards your spine, and through a 5-second count, begin to roll each vertebra off the floor, starting from your neck while simultaneously squeezing your knees together. Hold this sustained tension for a 5-second count and return to the starting position through a further 5-second count.

➔ preparation: hold this stretch for 15-20 seconds each side

Level 1

Complete 1 set of 10 repetitions.

Total = 10 repetitions

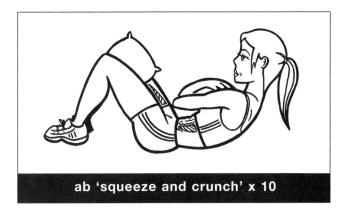

ab 'squeeze and crunch' x 10

Maximum time to complete the set: **3 minutes**

Level 2

Complete 1 set of 20 repetitions.

Total = 20 repetitions

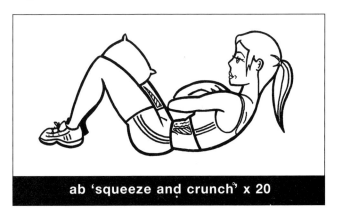

ab 'squeeze and crunch' x 20

Maximum time to complete the set: **5 minutes**

Level 3

Complete 1 set of 20 repetitions and 1 minute of skipping. Repeat.

Total = 20 repetitions

ab 'squeeze and crunch' x 20

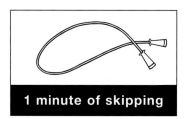

1 minute of skipping

REPEAT

Maximum time to complete the set: **7.5 minutes**

EXERCISE 3
MyoKinetics plyometric push-up and cat stretch
LEVELS 1 - 3

EXERCISE 3
MyoKinetics plyometric push-up and cat stretch

The plyometric push-up uses the same range of movement and muscle focus as the basic push-up, but we will be starting at the 'top' of the movement with arms outstretched, and finishing each repetition with an explosive ascent, as practised in a previous task. (Remember: NEVER lock your elbows. Keep them bent throughout this movement to avoid joint stress.)

From the starting position, lower your chest through a 5-second count towards the floor, holding the sustained tension (just above the floor) for a further 5-second count. From this position, focus on 'exploding' upwards with enough power to enable a slight lift of your hands off the floor. When your hands make contact with the floor, gently pull your hips backwards, leaving your palms on the floor and arms outstretched in front of you, until your bottom reaches your heels. Breathe deeply and lengthen your torso. Imagine that you are stretching for something just out of reach with your fingers. You should feel a stretch in your back, chest and shoulders as you hold this stretch for a count of 15 seconds.

➡ preparation: hold this cat stretch for 30 seconds

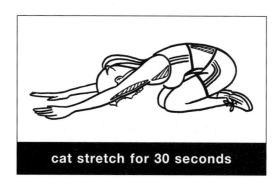

cat stretch for 30 seconds

Level 1

Complete 1 set of 6 repetitions, alternating each repetition with a cat stretch.

Total = 6 repetitions and 6 x 15 second stretches

pylometric push-up x 1

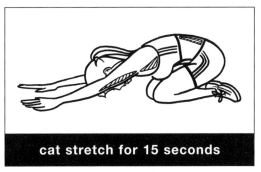

cat stretch for 15 seconds

REPEAT 5 TIMES

Maximum time to complete the set: **3.5 minutes**

Level 2

Complete 1 set of 12 repetitions, alternating every second repetition with a cat stretch.

Total = 12 repetitions and 6 cat stretches

pylometric push-up x 1

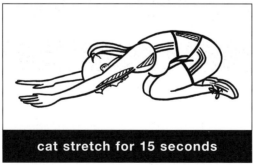

cat stretch for 15 seconds

REPEAT 11 TIMES

Maximum time to complete the set: **5 minutes**

Level 3

Complete 2 sets of 8 repetitions in the advanced push-up position (on your toes, knees off the floor), alternating every second repetition with a cat stretch. Skip for 1 minute after completing each set.

Total = 16 repetitions, 8 cat stretches and 2 minutes of skipping

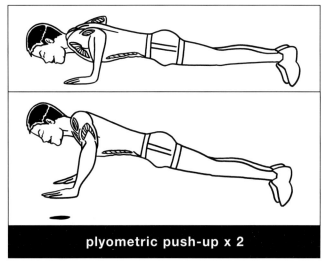

plyometric push-up x 2

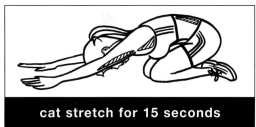

cat stretch for 15 seconds

REPEAT 3 TIMES

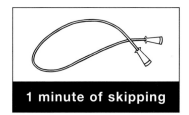

1 minute of skipping

REPEAT THIS ENTIRE COMBINATION TO COMPLETE 2 FULL SETS

Maximum time allowance to complete the set: **8 minutes**

EXERCISE 4
MyoKinetics glute bridge and stretch

As the name suggests, this exercise is great for deep-tissue glute toning, but it is also a compound movement putting our core stability to the test, as well as creating sustained tension on numerous muscle groups. Lying on your back, bend both knees and with your feet flat on the floor, bring your heels close to your bottom. Lift your right leg and rest the outside of your ankle against your left knee. With your hand by your sides and your palms flat on the floor, set your core stability and, through a 5-second count, push through your left heel to raise your torso off the floor. Hold the position of sustained tension for a 5-second count and slowly lower for 5 seconds, remembering your breathing and keeping your navel pulled tight towards your spine. Besides the total body muscle 'burn' you will experience, you will feel a strong stretch in your right glute and a strong contraction in the left glute. Repeat your total repetitions on this side before changing to the opposite side.

➡ preparation: hold this stretch for 20-30 seconds on each leg

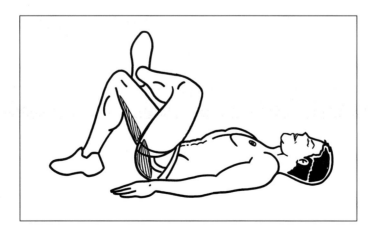

Level 1

Complete 1 set of 8 repetitions on each side.

Total = 16 repetitions

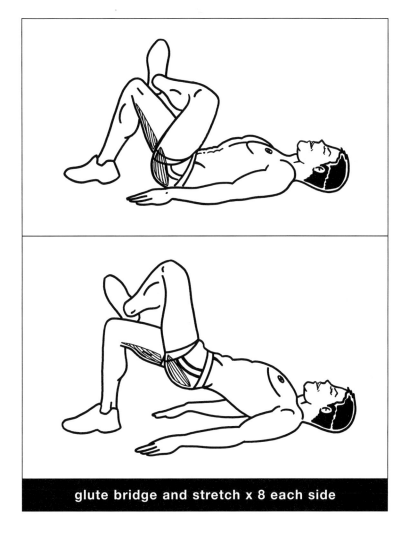

glute bridge and stretch x 8 each side

Maximum time allowance to complete the set: **4.5 minutes**

Level 2

Complete 1 set of 12 repetitions on each side.

Total = 24 repetitions

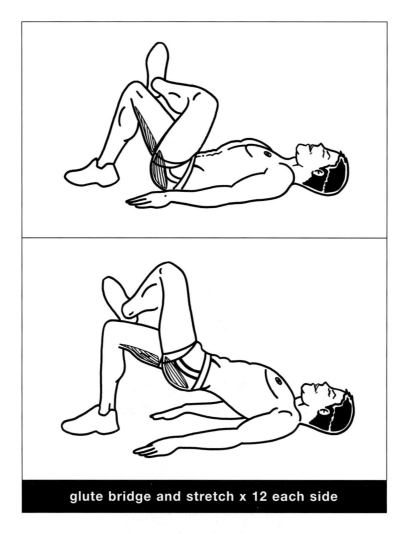

glute bridge and stretch x 12 each side

Maximum time allowance to complete the set: **6.5 minutes**

Level 3

Complete 2 sets of 12 repetitions and skip for 1 minute between each set.

Total = 24 repetitions and 1 minute of skipping

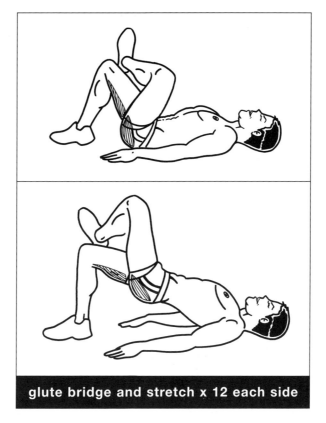

glute bridge and stretch x 12 each side

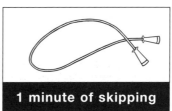

1 minute of skipping

REPEAT

Maximum time to complete the set: **8.5 minutes**

THE SHAPE OF THINGS TO COME...

Many of you have a burning desire to change your body, yet can't seem to muster the motivation to get started. While creating this book I have kept this in mind, to the point where you don't even have to leave home to begin!

If you can make the small step of putting aside some of your previous negative exercise experiences and give *MyoKinetics* a try, I have no doubt that you will not only create the desired results, but enjoy the process of seeing your body change before your very eyes.

Remember the three golden rules:

➔ Pace yourself

➔ Be consistent

➔ Focus, focus, focus!

The bottom line? You absolutely can *Look Good Naked* ... with confidence.

If you want to be kept up-to-date with Donna's latest work, you can register on her website at: www.DonnaAston.com, *or email her web manager at*: info@donnaaston.com.

Donna